WOMEN LEADERS

With Inspiring Stories

Naghilia Desravines

WomELLE

Featuring 10 bestseller, award-winning and up-and-coming authors:

Trina Ramsey

Kirsten Blakemore

Rhonda Kinard

Maggie Georgopoulos

Leslie Thomas Flowers

Tracie L. James

Divya Parekh

Rose Jones

Laura McNeill

Dr. Catherine Hayes.

Book design by Atmane Laouati.

First U.S. edition 2018

Library of Congress Control Number 2018912075

ISBN 978-0-9904531-3-0

eBook ISBN 978-0-9904531-4-7

PRINTED AND BOUND IN UNITED STATES OF AMERICA.

Dedication

To those women seeking help,

to those offering help,

and to all that opening businesses and leading.

Acknowledgments

Writing is never an easy effort, and as always, there are many people I have to thank for having the energy and ability to complete this anthology. At the top of the list, of course, is my son, Shem. More than anything, he keeps my purpose alive and all things in life that are important. My sincere thanks to Atmane Laouati for his support, encouragement, for the hand-holding, the listening, the sympathy, the empathy and for being the inner circle. Friends in need, friends indeed. Rose Jones, my friend, is another of the many blessings in my life. Seasons and men come and go, but girlfriends are forever.

Divya Parekh and Rhonda Kinard, for your extreme supports and patience. You all know what your contributions were. My mind and body thank you.

And finally, I owe many debts of gratitude to all my contributors, WomELLE board of directors, colleagues, friends, critics, and family members. I thank my contributors ———, you'll find their stories inspiring and motivating.

About the author

Naghilia Desravines is a mother, Founder and CEO of WomELLE, a community that specializes in programs that motivate and inspire women. Naghilia has a master's degree in Psychology, currently pursuing a PhD in Psychology. She has over twelve years of experience as an entrepreneur with many corporate leadership positions. She is the author of Cold Hearted, a novel published in 2014. Naghilia has a unique way to motivate and inspire women of all ages. Her approach, titled "The 3 C's of life: Choices. Chances. Changes" inspires a message that resonates with emerging women and groups wanting to achieve more; it gives them the tools they need to succeed.

Naghilia believes that women must make a choice to take a chance or their life will never change.

You can find her on the Web at www.naghiliadesravines.com or visit www.womelle.com.

Sometimes following your heart means going your own way, even if the path gets lonely and hard.

Naghilia Desravines

CONTENTS

WOMEN LEADERS

With Inspiring Stories

An Anthology

The Inspiring Story of Ten Women Leaders

Maya Angelou once proudly said, "I am grateful to be a woman, I must have done something great in another life." You can hear my resounding agreement with Miss Angelou—just being a woman and taking ownership of your life is enough to qualify as a successful woman!

A woman in today's world can define herself in ways that might not have been possible a century or even some decades ago. Nowadays, a woman can stand on the shoulders of giants, such as Michelle Obama, and use their courage and strength as role models for themselves. A woman in this century is a power player juggling many roles with confidence and panache because she has learned to harness her core qualities to play several parts simultaneously. Being a woman entails having the essential attributes of being comfortable in her skin irrespective of the judgment meted out by the world around her. Nevertheless, the road to emancipation has been rocky. Some of the challenges that women have faced in the past continue to create obstacles to the progress of women as they carve out their career and life path.

A woman is always working. She works in the house, does the chores, feeds the kids and manages the finances; however, these are not counted as gainful employment. If she chooses to work outside the home, she will have to face the problem of balancing a job with household work and child rearing, which are responsibilities that are traditionally handed over to women. A woman who chooses to work has additional barriers she must face, such as workplace abuse, inequitable pay, the pressure to conform to traditional gender roles, and the lack of affordable childcare.

The gender divide is one of the biggest challenges for women trying to get ahead in their careers. Equal pay and opportunities to succeed may be visible on the horizon of employers and organizations, but it has not translated into a perceptible change in the day-to-day treatment of women. All over the world, women still struggle with issues of gender discrimination, fair pay, and violation of dignity. The International Labor Organization lists the labor force participation of women in the world as 48.7% as opposed to the much higher 75.2% statistic of working men; this gaping divide can be attributed to the lack of similar educational and job opportunities as men. Virginia Woolf, a writer with a sensitive mind, had termed the lack of women writers as "empty spaces on bookshelves." Thus, there are similar empty spaces in workplaces today that need to be filled by women.

It comes as no surprise that statistics all over the globe show that women occupy a minority of the top-ranking positions in companies and businesses. So, what's stopping them? In a scenario of male-dominance and unequal opportunities for women, tremendous self-confidence and courage are required for a woman to step forward and break out of conventional molds. Women not only have to work extremely hard at their jobs to scale the ranks—they have to go one better than the men around them, and what's more, they have to deal with prejudice based on gender in the workplace. In addition, women who are mothers are viewed as less committed as compared to their male counterparts. Men do not have to deal with such pre-conceived notions, and their work performance is interpreted per se. If a woman raises an opinion at work or shows traits off leadership such as assertiveness and self-assurance, she is viewed as a "bully," "bossy" or a "shrew". A woman's competence and confidence are not desired attributes in the workplace; she is simply expected to agree with the opinions of male colleagues and bosses, without the freedom to express independent ideas.

Are men the only ones who stereotype women? The ugly truth is that women are also accomplices to that affront because they do not act as an anchor for their female peers. Although a female boss or colleague can be expected to be sensitive to the struggles faced by other female executives, the reality is that women in power sometimes bully other women, even more than men. Why do women feel the need to cut down other women instead of supporting them? Women in power may often feel the need to conform to the behavior of their male peers, or be reluctant to express overt feminist opinions. The need to fit in, or to hold onto hard-won power may be some of the underlying factors that prevent women from empathizing with women co-workers. Sadly, the attitude of treating other women as enemies destroys their confidence and defeats the core values of diversity and inclusion in an organization. If a woman wants to move *up the ladder in a skirt* (I have borrowed that term from Maggie Georgopoulos'book title), she will have to confront the insecurities and intolerant attitude of both men and women. Furthermore, when men observe women treating other women poorly, it strengthens their belief in their inability to succeed at their jobs.

What does it take for a woman to become a leader and overcome the formidable resistance to her success? If a person aspires to occupy a top executive position or take on a leadership role in business, he or she needs to develop the core qualities of competence, vision, hard work and perseverance. However, for a woman, there is an added dimension as well—the ability to overpower hurdles at the workplace with courage

4

and self-belief. The problems encountered in the workplace may take the form of power struggles, unequal opportunities for growth, biased opinions on gender roles, or financial hardships. Women in leadership roles empower themselves through their struggles; nevertheless, their responsibility towards women does not end there. The goal of women empowerment does not stop when one woman achieves her life goals; the torch of empowerment needs to be passed on from one woman to another, igniting a virtual forest fire of motivation among women all around. Michelle Obama, a long-time champion of women's rights has said, "As women, we must stand up for ourselves. As women, we must stand up for each other. And finally, as women, we must stand up for justice for all."

| | |

Women leaders—CEOs, entrepreneurs, executives and so on— who have made it to the top of their careers have unlocked the secrets of sustained success and are now able to guide others achieve their goals. I believe that the best way to learn is from the ones that are already there. This book will take you through the extraordinary journey of ten women leaders who I had the pleasure to meet in the past few years. Through our talks and interaction, I was lucky enough to get a glimpse of their lives through their own eyes. These women have strived hard to reach where they are today—at the forefront of their careers. I discovered that each one of them has a story to tell, a narrative of experiences strung together by threads of unwavering belief in her abilities. Let me unravel these personas just a little with a few opening lines...

First, we have Trina Ramsey who is the kind of person that will make you want to be more—more than you are right now and more than you think you can be. She is an executive, career and life strategist, motivational speaker and writer, and the founder of the Just Do You Institute. This institute is a platform for women empowerment, which is a theme very close to my heart. Her institute helps women in their 40s, 50s and even 60s get the support they need to launch their careers. As I spoke to Trina, I began to see what makes her story stand out from others. Trina leads the way by her remarkable personal journey as she transformed her life and started her coaching business in 2009. Additionally, she has kept a personal journal since she was a teenager and recently decided to pen down her perspectives about life. She went on to compile her thoughts into a book and is currently the celebrated author of *Just Do You! A Declaration of Independence from Guilt, Obligation and Shame*. She has also contributed to another bestseller called *The Art of UnLearning: Top Experts Share Personal Stories on the Power of Perseverance*. Trina is a fearless woman who believes life is too short to ruminate on what-ifs. Interacting with Trina made me want to explore my own limitless potential—such is the motivating effect she has on those around her!

The next power woman I spoke to was Kirsten Blakemore. Her credentials are long—she is an MA, CPCC, ACC, CHC and Senior Consulting Partner at *Partners in Leadership*, and a *Forbes Coaches Council* member. If that is not impressive enough, she is also a prolific author, speaker, and executive mentor with many years of experience as a woman leader in the field of sales and marketing. As I learned more about her, I began to see her as a superwoman of sorts. She uses her superpowers of expertise, genuineness and motivational skills to help executives and top organizations, to resolve issues that hinder their progress. A superheroine who has made helping other women her life goal, Kirsten regularly publishes articles and blog posts on how women can work through power struggles and the gender divide and emerge successfully. She holds an undergraduate business degree and a Master's degree in Psychology—a winning combination that she uses to help other executives push ahead in their careers.

If you are struggling to achieve a goal, Rhonda Kinard is the person to seek out. She is the CEO of *A Life Ignited, LLC*, an organization that helps people and teams to ignite their inner fire and achieve their personal and professional goals. Even professionals and top executives sometimes feel they are in a rut and their careers are not moving forward. This is where Rhonda excels, as she is skilled in motivating people and teams and propelling them towards their aims; her motto is that consistent action can lead to sustained success. I asked

Rhonda during our interactions about what fuels her inner fire and keeps her motivated, to which she responded that unwavering self-care is the mortar in the bricks, and that without it, the house of leadership collapses. Her passion, drive, and unapologetic self-confidence are truly inspiring. Rhonda is also a motivational speaker and the author of *A Life Ignited - Ignite Your Inner Fuse*, where she shared her personal successes and setbacks to use them as an inspiration for others on how to tackle adversity and emerge with shining colors.

Maggie Georgopoulos is a go-getter—she knows what she wants and more importantly, how to get it. She is a globally acknowledged authority for women on navigating male-dominated workspaces and expertly juggles many roles as an author, consultant, speaker, and trainer. She has written the bestseller book *Up the Ladder in a Skirt*, which shows women how to take the reins of their career in their hands. Maggie comes across as a highly motivated and driven person who, in her own words, is always looking for her next adventure. Her insight about her personality helps her sustain a career that is fulfilling and suits her personality type. This is the message she likes to convey as a career consultant and trainer as she encourages executives to identify their personality type and choose career paths that nurture their specific preferences. Maggie is also a champion for mental health and its role in the workplace, having authored the book *Mental Health is NOT a Dirty Word*, which talks about how to change misconceptions surrounding mental health in the workplace. Maggie is a woman leader, but that is not enough for her. She is an advocate for women leadership, and her efforts have helped more than 10,000 women in over 32 countries ascend the ladder of success.

I have often seen women in my line of work suffering from a lack of assertiveness. The existing pay gap gets wider each time a woman does not speak up for what her job is worth. Sometimes women get molded into becoming people-pleasers without appreciating the value of their position in an organization. That is why Leslie Thomas Flowers is changing the game for women who need that extra push to stand up for themselves. She is a trailblazer for women in business—she helps women take charge of their career and balance it successfully with their personal life. Talking to Leslie made me feel that women can have it all! Her Mastermind program shows women practical ways by which they can pursue their dreams and turn it into a lucrative business. She also is the bestselling author of the highly motivational books *Kettle-Dreams: Mastermind Guide to Think and Grow Rich and Own your Purpose and Realize your Potential.* Leslie is the wind beneath the wings of many women entrepreneurs, and they now soar higher than they ever thought they could.

Does zero mean the absence of something essential? I thought so too before I met Tracie L. James; she redefined the meaning of zero for me. Tracie says that she is on a "Mission to Zero"—zero excuses and more results! Tracie believes in the simple principle of making individuals and teams *excuse-proof*, instead of *excuse-laden*. It is possible to create a high-performing team when people are accountable, which directly translates to more profits and productivity. Talking to Tracie made it clear to me that the vision of one person can lead to a significant transformation for countless others struggling for direction. Tracie is a leadership strategist with over 20 years of diverse experience in leadership development, managing accounts, sales, and political campaign planning. She is a multi-talented power woman and seamlessly shifts between the roles of author, speaker, writer, and consultant. Her recently released book is titled *Excuse Proof Leadership*, which is also the theme of the Masterclass courses she runs for leadership development. Tracie calls herself an "Agent Zero" and that means the presence of everything needed to succeed.

A seed grows into a plant all on its own. However, what if someone nurtures it? The seed will most likely take the form of a flourishing tree and spreads its roots everywhere. An entrepreneur develops a business independently, but his or her growth may not progress adequately without a mentor to propel it further than originally conceived. Divya Parekh has been in the business of helping business take that leap to success with her unique strategies for many years now. Her USP is her emphasis on how leaders, teams, and entrepreneurs can build relationships and connections with people using a 9-step science-based growth process developed by her. I asked Divya how individuals and organizations could cultivate success and engage their employees, and she told me that the answers could be found in her many bestselling books that have brought her global recognition. She believes in people and their inherent potential for success. Her motivational, coaching, and leadership talks can be all that is needed for an individual or an organization to realize their vision and reach the next stage of achievement.

Women leaders need to fortify themselves to face a work environment that does very little to nurture self-confidence. It is possible to look for motivation to push past obstacles from colleagues, bosses, and others; however, why put your emotional well-being into another person's hands? Rose Jones is a certified Life and Accountability coach who shows women that the key to self-development is looking within, not without. She uses the powerful tool of reflection to help women empower themselves by reflecting on how their thought process works and, more importantly, how to modify it for life enhancement. Rose feels that it is essential to look into the mirror and confront your past mistakes, overcome fears and dig deep within to explore your potential. Through our talks, I discovered that Rose also addresses social issues such as domestic violence. She works extensively with single mothers and young women who often need a nudge to take charge of their life. She is a believer in self-sufficiency and is currently running her coaching business called *Let Rose Speak* while conducting online training, workshops and motivational lectures.

Laura McNeill is an adjunct professor at Samford University's Design and Technology graduate program, a Ph.D. candidate at the University of Alabama's College of Education, Department of Educational Leadership, Policy, and Technology, and instructional designer for Regions Bank in Birmingham. I certainly did not expect someone so qualified and proficient to describe herself on her website simply as "a mother, daughter, friend, thinker, and lover of all things pink". That is Laura McNeill for you—a down-to-Earth person who multitasks effortlessly and succeeds at every role she plays! She is not just a top gear researcher and educator but also the bestselling author of many bestselling works of fiction under her name and a pen name *Lauren Clark*. She is a role model for young students who are learning the ropes about diversity, equity, leadership, and technology that gives them the tools needed to become formidable leaders of tomorrow. I found her well-balanced and creative persona the most impressive trait that shows people around her that it is possible to achieve fulfillment through diverse career paths.

Enneagram is an ancient tool for identifying a person's personality type. Even though it has been around for centuries, most people do not realize how the Enneagram can be a powerful personal transformative tool. Dr. Catherine Hayes, a certified Executive Coach teacher, alongside the *International Enneagram Association*, has helped people give their life a do-over. "It's time to change your life," she says. Catherine is a highly qualified influencer in the arena of leadership, having occupied several leadership roles in local, national, and international organizations. A natural motivator and speaker, she is immensely passionate about Enneagram coaching, which she conducts privately and within organizations as well. Catherine discussed her harsh childhood with me, and it gave me insight into her indomitable persona. She has chronicled her inspiring life journey in the bestselling book *Everything is Going to Be Okay! From the Projects to Harvard to Freedom*, which shows how it is possible to rise from despair to the pinnacle of success.

To become an icon for women empowerment through leadership is a daunting task, indeed, but not an impossible one. History is replete with examples of women powering through adversity and emerging at the top. The boss women I talked to showed me that it is possible to have a dream and make it work while enjoying the roles of a mother, wife, daughter, and so on. I thoroughly enjoyed getting a glimpse of their lives and understanding what makes them who they are. These ten women leaders own each aspect of themselves and certainly do not need the world to tell them how fantastic they are.

Michelle Obama once urged women to "Always stay true to yourself and never let what somebody says distract you from your goals."Talking, sharing and reading these inspiring stories will help you do just that. Through this book, I hope you derive the joy and delight that I received through my sessions with these amazing women in equal measure. The next chapters will hopefully pave the way for women taking baby steps into the big bad world and give them the confidence and encouragement to achieve their career and life goals.

Chapter 1

Lessons in leadership from a supermom entrepreneur

Trina Ramsey

T his is a message from a seasoned veteran to my younger sisters. You may be a rising star at your office, a working mom, a mentee, or just starting out in your career. If you see yourself in these descriptions, this section is just for you!

Since my niche is career and executive coaching, I will use my own story to share a few lessons that I have learned that profoundly affected my life and my career. Women in leadership are common, but we face many interesting obstacles that our male counterparts don't have to take into consideration. I have often said, "I wish I knew then what I know now." However, I also realize that the challenges we face in life are the things that help us to grow. Facing down adversity and finding a way to win in difficult circumstances shows us what we're really made of and gives us proof that we've got what it takes to succeed the next time the going gets tough.

My career path has been full and varied. I have always been

a "seeker" of wisdom and sources of positivity. Long before I had an inkling to become a coach, I was devouring material by thought leaders like Steven Covey, Iyanla Vansant and Anthony Robbins. I always wanted to make a difference in the world; therefore, despite having a bachelor's degree in Information Systems and landing a terrific job at IBM in the 80s, I walked away from it three years later. I felt like a cog in a huge corporate machine, where the bottom line was sales and profitability. Now I realize that I had already encountered one of my core philosophies about work – that you spend so much time working that it is important for it to be enjoyable or feel meaningful to you. I didn't come to this realization until years later.

I'm getting ahead of myself. To be fair, I got some of the best sales training in my life while I was at IBM. Having "Big Blue" on my résumé has helped me tremendously; however, after being there for a while, I knew that I would not retire from that company. I needed to contribute and connect with people; and I got to do that as an IBM volunteer, which is where I had my first experience volunteering with Habitat for Humanity. I had no idea at the time that destiny would lead me to work for that amazing organization and lead a fundraising team to build houses in the Nation's Capital. It remains one of my most fulfilling jobs ever. While working for IBM, I also mentored and tutored youth, which I found tremendously rewarding, and planted the seeds for a career contributing to the greater good.

Three years in at IBM, I got the itch to do something more. Therefore, I left before the "golden handcuffs" took hold and have never regretted it. My first stop was to launch my own interior decorating business, which was a lot of fun. Becoming an entrepreneur in my 20s is one of my proudest moments. I didn't realize until later what a big risk I was taking. It just felt natural.

After I had been running my decorating business for a couple of years, we were blessed with a beautiful baby girl. Like many parents, I was completely unprepared for the level of demands that would come from this tiny person. It was difficult to manage taking care of a newborn, making sales calls and overseeing paint projects, furniture deliveries and window dressing installations. It was hard to keep the money coming in given the unpredictable pace of it all, so it was time to get a job again. That was when I reinvented myself the second time and became a non-profit fundraiser, a career I have thrived at for over 20 years.

However, I wasn't yet done with my journey. In 2009, I responded to a call that I had ignored several years before and began pursuing my coaching career. The mix of skills and experiences I gained along the way had already been preparing me for what I now know is my true purpose in life.

Sometimes I marvel at the hand of God in my life. Seemingly unrelated events, people and opportunities provided the roadmap necessary to put me where I am today. It has been an incredible ride, and I am profoundly grateful. Of course, I have endured my bumps and bruises along the way, which have all helped me to become the woman I am today. My kids are young adults now, but these lessons also helped me as a parent, for each stage of their development began a new learning curve for me. I've been divorced for over 10 years now, but the concept of "supermom" became even more real as I navigated the murky waters of single parenthood and co-parenting.

| | |

Below are just a few of the truths I've gleaned from my journey.

The Three A's of Leadership: Authenticity. Action. Accountability.

I am a natural leader. As the eldest of three girls, I earned the title *Mini-mom* early on. When my mother died when I was fourteen and my sisters were seven, my road to independence accelerated. As I matured into adulthood, I began building a successful track record and was naturally selected to lead clubs and work groups. I became superwoman—a role that is familiar to many of us. However, there were times when I didn't appreciate the role, and I struggled with it over the years. I have journaled, blogged and spoken about the complexities and pitfalls that befall those of us who wear the cape, and about how we can give ourselves permission to set it aside when it no longer serves us. Being a working mom makes the juggle even more precarious, but it's worth it. I wouldn't trade any of my roles or stops along the way.

There is a lot I can say about leadership, but I decided to share three practices that I find most important for leaders that have taken me far in life, and that I admire most in my mentors, sisterpreneurs and role models.

Authenticity

I spent many years trying to run from a shameful past. I tried to fit into other people's boxes and live up to their expectations of me. Thus, when I first became a coach, I tried to project a sanitized version of myself to keep myself safe from public humiliation. Nevertheless, what I didn't realize was that I was being inauthentic by doing so. I was trying to show a perfect superwoman who never had any problems, when the reality was far from that. Truth be told, I still harboured several insecurities, even as I was launching my career as a coach. Nine years later, I have learned to be myself. I was embraced by several mentors and invested in myself through coaching and leadership training. Some wise women helped me to recognize my own greatness, rather than run from it or diminish my personal power. Now I have found my tribe and I have learned to speak with truth, openness and vulnerability. I know who I am, and I know who I'm not; I no longer come across generic the way I used to. I show people my true self—a woman with a big heart and some battle scars. I am a woman who has been there and done that. I have learned some lessons from falling down and getting back up, and I am no longer afraid of sharing the pain, struggle and hardships that I have endured, as well as the difficulties that I still face from time to time.

When I look at the people I admire most, this trait of authenticity shines through time and time again.

I think of Maya Angelou, who spent a lifetime sharing her story boldly and authentically, and empowering countless women around the world by speaking her truth and providing words for the rest of us when we had none to share. The poem *Phenomenal Woman* is a tribute to women everywhere—the power, the beauty and poise that we all have access to, but rarely claim as our own.

Oprah Winfrey is also a wonder. One of the things I love about her is how she shares her journey with us all. Despite being a billionaire, she talks about the difficulties she has faced in life, including her struggles with abuse and weight loss. She even shares with us the people who have supported her along the way so that we can also grow and climb.

I recently spent time with one of my mentors, Sylvia High. She exudes authenticity. She is vibrant, warm, and there is not one phony thing about her. I recently attended her *I Am Woman* conference, and the grace, passion and pure love with which she conducted the entire weekend was very inspiring. I am grateful that I get to have her in my life; she has made a difference for many people. It appears she does it effortlessly, but I know that she pours her entire being into her work, not because she has to, but because she cares.

Action

I have never been a stranger to hard work. I was a star performer at IBM and though my career there was short, I earned the coveted "100 percent club" each year, and a fabulous trip to go along with it. Starting my first business when I was in my 20s taught me many lessons about life and leadership; it's where I first learned that working for yourself meant selling yourself. Sales is an excellent training ground for being in action. I worked home shows, made cold calls, and honed my sales pitch. I learned that you had to get a lot of noes to get to a yes, and not to take noes personally. I also learned about prioritizing my work and how to wear many hats simultaneously.

I went on to build a track record of success as a non-profit fundraiser for over 20 years. Each year the slate is wiped clean and you have a new set of financial goals to pursue, or the good work of the organization does not happen, and people don't get paid. No pressure! My sales training at IBM prepared me to approach and manage goals, seek the "win/win" in business relationships, and connect with my clients or donors to find out what motivates them and show them how what I have to offer helps them to achieve their philanthropic or other goals.

All these skills enabled me to have the nerve to pursue yet another career as a life coach. Since that day ten years ago when I embraced the dream, I have hosted workshops and retreats, launched several product lines, and become a two-time best-selling author and international speaker. Years ago, when I was a sales rep at IBM in my tailored suits, I would have never believed these achievements were possible for me. I am grateful for my journey and the many blessings that have come along the way, but I am also grateful for the times that things didn't go as planned, and the lessons learned from each of those experiences.

The one common denominator to my success in life and leadership is staying in action. Once I decided to do something, I created a plan and then executed it. When things didn't go well, I regrouped and went at it again. As a coach, I get a lot of satisfaction from teaching my clients these skills so that they can pursue their dreams.

The only way you can truly get things done is to act. Take one step, then another, and then another.

Also, don't try to go it alone. An African proverb states, "If you want to go fast, go alone. If you want to go far, go together." It is very tempting for us superwomen to try to do things all by ourselves. We don't ask for help; we "never let 'em see us sweat". It's bullshit. Sorry—I had to say it. We've been programmed to back ourselves into a corner and isolate, rather than share the load and seek support. I have found that having a community of friends, fellow coaches and others to share the journey with, eases the burden and makes the journey a more joyous one. We get to have fun and connect with people even while we are climbing the ladder of success.

Accountability

This is one of the most powerful tools in my coach's toolkit. If you want to make sure you do something—tell someone. If you really want to go big—tell a lot of people. It will keep you honest and boost your likelihood of succeeding.

Accountability is what makes the difference between a wish and a dream; it is a key ingredient that helps us put our butt on the line. Sometimes it's about not wanting to let someone down. Unfortunately, this has roots in being a people-pleaser, which is not the best motivation. Sometimes we are too concerned about our reputation. We pride ourselves on getting things done, and if we say we're going to do something, we're more likely to follow through with it than trying to motivate ourselves alone.

My role as a coach is primarily that of an accountability partner. When I work with my clients, whether 1-on-1 or as part of a group, I regularly check in on how my clients are following through on the plans they have made. I work with them to see what is working, what is not, and how to get past whatever is blocking them.

As leaders, it's important to hold ourselves accountable. Depending on what your work situation is, this may be built into the work, or it may be something that you have to create systems or structures for yourself to achieve your goals. I spent over 20 years as a non-profit fundraising, a profession that has built in accountability. There is nothing like revenue goals and targets to keep you honest and in forward motion; it's a good path for someone who is goal-oriented and likes a challenge.

On the other hand, entrepreneurship is a very unstructured path that requires high degrees of self-motivation and accountability. It's important to build a reputation of doing what you say you're going to do; the more you prove to yourself and others that your word means something, the more natural of a habit it becomes. I highly recommend either joining or starting a mastermind group, which is a group of peers who have similar goals and connect regularly via phone, in person, or virtually in order to pursue those goals. It has built-in accountability, as well as networking benefits.

Embracing the Three A's in your life

Here is a little guide to help you become more successful and fulfilled in your life through the use of authenticity, action and accountability. Do you have a journal? This section is a good place to take notes for yourself. Dig in and see what emerges.

Do some self-examination. Make plans. Try out some ideas.

Authenticity

When is the last time that you took time to reflect on who you are and what you are meant to be in the world? How does it align with how you show up? Do people naturally "get" you? Do your words match your actions? Do you ever find yourself saying things that you don't believe? Do you feel like you are living a lie? These questions will help you really check in with yourself and consider how authentically you are showing up in the world. Take some time to journal about what's not working for you, and how you can change it.

I will admit that there were times in my life when I was feeling like a fraud. I was not being real with people, and only showed this confident face that we superwomen are so good at portraying. Even in my marriage, my ex-husband and I had cultivated this reputation as "the perfect couple". We weren't being honest with ourselves about who we were and the challenges we faced, let alone everyone else! In the end, when the marriage fell apart after 17 years, it kept us from keeping the charade going. While it was shocking and painful at the time, now that I look back at it, I realize that I had begun painting myself into a corner and shrinking myself to fulfill an image that I didn't fit. In *WomELLE* magazine, I recently wrote an article entitled, *How my divorce helped me embrace my life's calling*. Don't get me wrong, I want every relationship to succeed, and it took me over 10 years to realize that had I stayed in that relationship, I might not have allowed myself to pursue my true calling of becoming a coach, author and motivational speaker. Unfortunately, I am still single… I'm not a relationship coach after all, but I have never been felt freer and more comfortable in my own skin than when I decided to follow my heart and embrace this part of my life.

Even as a coach, it's been a journey for me to let go of the mask and allow myself to speak freely about some of the unpleasant things about my past, mistakes I've made, and my own doubts, fears and insecurities. Since I embraced my tribe of 40, 50 and 60-somethings at the Just Do You Institute for Women's Empowerment, I've learned to be more open, transparent, and real. And it has truly made all the difference.

Action

Are you a person who takes action, or do you procrastinate? Are there things that you want to achieve, but haven't found the nerve to pursue? How does fear of failure and success influence your ability to make things happen? Pull out your journal and write about it.

Some of you reading this are women who get things done. Period. I know you. I am you. Don't let life pass you by while you are busy achieving your goals. Spend time with your family and friends. Take trips. Enjoy life because we only get one, and it passes very quickly!

Here are a few ways to upgrade your game and take action on a regular basis:

1. Start.

It's really that simple. Some of us get stuck in analysis paralysis and can't get out the gate because we are so busy planning for every eventuality that we kill our own momentum before we even get started. What is one thing that you want to achieve? What is the first step that you need to take to make that happen? Do that. What is the next step? Do that. Repeat. Go forth!

2. Break down your goals into smaller chunks.

Take it one step at a time. Don't let the size of the goal deter you from starting.

3. Get organized.

I have always been an organizer junkie. I love planners, notebooks, and the like. Lately, I've been enjoying the simple flexibility of using bullet journals. Some days all I need is a list of the 3-5 top things that I need to accomplish, and other days I need to map out months—long projects, with action steps, deadlines and milestones. Find what works for you and come up with a way to keep things organized, including your time.

4. Gather your team.

Depending on how big the goal is, you need someone in your corner to make it happen. Maybe you need to hire help, like a virtual or real-life assistant. Maybe you need a coach, mastermind team or mentor. Maybe you just need someone you trust to share your dream with, who will be your cheerleader, and help you stay motivated when the going gets rough, as it inevitably will at times.

5. Stay in forward motion.

Do something every day to get you closer to your goal. *Every day.* Make it a part of your routine to work on your goal and you will be more likely to stay on target.

6. Live a little!

Some of us are super intense and need to take a break, so make sure you are having fun along the way.

Accountability

In my journey, I have had people at each stage helping me to stay grounded and in action. No matter how good leader you are, it's important to surround yourself with people who are like-minded. Seek out mentors and role models who have already achieved what you would like to do. Their guidance will prove invaluable.

When I was writing my first book, my publisher Kim

Brown of Minerva Rising Press played that role for me. She knew the business of book publishing, and she helped me map out the plan. She coached me on my writing, so that the product was something that I am truly proud of, and she helped me stay mindful of deadlines and worked through the many rounds of editing and revision necessary to make the project a reality. I am eternally grateful for her leadership and expertise.

Here are a few ways to stay accountable to yourself or others:

1. Go public.

Tell your goal to someone. Start with a close circle or recruit an accountability partner to keep you honest. This works very well with health and fitness goals but can also work with other enterprises.

2. Share the journey.

As I was embarking upon my coaching career, my good friend Marva was training to become a health coach. Though we were pursuing different disciplines, we decided to become study partners, sitting together occasionally to do our work or brainstorm on business ideas. In between our study sessions, we would call each other up whenever we got stuck or discouraged. Even though that was years ago, we still find each other, compare notes and celebrate one another's success. I am so grateful for her!

3. Hire help.

Get a coach, a business advisor, or someone else to help you get where you are going. Using a sports analogy, this is like hiring a personal trainer. We may make plans to go to the gym or for a run, and then allow ourselves to procrastinate or get too busy. On the contrary, if we have an appointment with someone who is as invested in our success as we are, we are much more likely to show up. Eventually, we may gain the discipline to do it on our own but having a trainer and seeing results can make a huge difference.

In closing, I encourage you to embrace life and all that it has to offer. Life is too short to second-guess yourself, play small or show up as someone other than who you already are. You are uniquely designed to do something special in this world, and you already have what it takes. I applaud you. I am rooting for you, and if there is anything that I can do to support you in your journey, please be sure to let me know.

Chapter 2

Victim or Victor? You choose

Kirsten Blakemore

O ur daily life is filled with conscious and unconscious choices. We can choose to yell at someone who cuts in front of us in the grocery store line, or calmly let them step in front of us. We can choose to eat at McDonalds frequently and then complain that we are overweight and not at fault, or not. Might we even be able to choose how our bodies manifest disease? It seems that our society is used to deal with more stress and pressure today than ever before. We work hard to make ends meet, saving money enough to pay the bills, pay for the kids' school, sports, arts, college and perhaps throw in a vacation every now and then. Oh, and let's include managing a partnership or marriage relationship. That does not even address the family drama that occurs… or maybe that's just mine.

So, how does one find balance? While I have written articles about that subject over the years that have been published, I believe I have gained a new perspective based on my experience.

My story begins where most do—at a young age. I recall being socially awkward. During elementary school, I have memories of being the last one chosen for the kickball team and, in addition, when it was my turn to kick the ball, I reinforced the reasons why I was picked last. I just couldn't seem to coordinate my body with any sport.

No one can say I didn't try, because I did. My mom enrolled me in ballet, which I did for several years, I participated in gymnastics, and was a figure skater. I can't say I was good at any of them, but I do recall having fun. In hindsight, those activities may have given me some grace that I completely lacked.

The problem I ran into with each of those activities was that I found myself being critical about my body; I did not conform to the shape of a good gymnast or ballerina, and I longed to be thin like them; however, physically speaking, I was a big girl. Even later in life, I had people say to me "Kirsten, you are just a big girl." And, yes, I hurt.

I grew up in a middle-class family, though we always seemed to be struggling for money. My mom was diligent about having healthy food around the house, much to the chagrin of my brother and me. Even so, I would find a way to get candy. When money was tight, and we needed food fast, we would go to McDonalds—I would get a Big Mac, French fries, milkshake, and sometimes a pie. Burger King was also an option; there I would order a Whopper Jr, fries and so on. I remember we used to eat donuts or cinnamon buns that my mom made on Sunday mornings as a treat before or after church. Naturally, my waist grew.

By junior high school, I began dieting. I started trying to exercise by either joining the cheerleading squad or playing after school. I tried running, but since I had asthma, that didn't work out for me so well. I remember trying out for the track and field team… One day at practice, the coach had us run around the track several times and I experienced an asthma attack that left me breathless. I was so embarrassed that I tried to pretend nothing was wrong; however, when I could no longer get a breath, I had to stop running. I was humiliated; it seemed as if everyone else was a gazelle and I was a pig, and I think pigs can run faster. I dropped out of track the next day. Did I mention I tried out for softball and hit myself in the face with the ball? I don't even know how I could have done that, but I did. Again, I left tryouts right after.

Finally, in high school, I joined the swim team. I was a natural in the water; I loved swimming and could work out for hours. Amazingly, I had no asthma attacks while swimming, and it was the only sport that I could feel good about myself. I could tell others felt that I was adding value to the team, so I strived to be the best. Each year I would try harder and continually improved. Nevertheless, my body was still "big." Somehow, I equated being big with a slower time. I would sometimes win swimming the 50 yard or 100-yard freestyle race, but when I lost, it was by seconds. Those seconds plagued my mind. All I wanted was to have a sport where I could be the best.

Seconds…I needed to cut off seconds.

Some of my friends at the time told me that if I really wanted to lose weight, I could just make myself throw up. Therefore, anytime I would eat, they would say, "Just throw it up after." I desperately wanted to lose weight, lose those seconds that could mean the difference between first and second place. However, I couldn't stop myself from eating because I loved food, so I began to throw up. Thus, began the mental and physical battle I had with my weight—I would criticize myself for eating, I would go throw up and then I would eat again. The cycle repeated itself so many times that I ended up being the co-captain of the swim team my senior year in high school. I did well and suffered quietly.

That was really the beginning of what became my strong interest—body image, food, exercise, and ultimately the balance among all three. What I didn't know back then was that purging probably had the opposite effect on my swim time; however, it did become a habit. It was the only way I could have control over my body and what I put into it. I am not certain of what was worse—the physical impact purging had on my body, or the mental anguish I inflicted on myself because of poor body image and self-esteem.

During that time, I modeled for local clothing companies. I loved dressing up in the clothing and modeling, as well as the runways, photo shoots and commercials. Ironically, I was working in a job where it was vital to have a certain body size. I had that size, indeed, but if you had asked me then if I thought I had a good shape, I would have said, "No, I need to lose 10 pounds." I was never good enough for me, so I continued the cycle from big to small to big using purging, then moving to eating very little. When people continued asking me how I planned to lose more weight, I began responding that by eating even less.

This is the inner battle that an out-of-whack body image will play. I had what I now refer to as "gremlins", or that critical voice in my head telling me how ugly and fat I was. Despite that, I continued finding myself in situations and jobs where my body was vital to the role! I modeled in New York City for a couple of years, and then moved to Los Angeles, where my clothing size increased four sizes. As my weight increased, my earning power decreased; I was losing out on work resulting from my weight gain. Not only was my inner critic working overtime, but also, I was having the message reinforced by lack of work.

At that time, agents suggested plus size modeling to accommodate my weight gain. I agreed and then the work rolled in! I was on the cover of *Big Beautiful Women* magazine, which established me in that category. While I was really happy to be working so frequently as a model, that happiness resulted in weight loss. I was then told I was too thin to work plus size anymore.

In my 20s and 30s, I would exercise frequently to quiet the critical voice. Sometimes I would go to the gym twice a day to quiet the negative, shaming voice and to lose those unwanted calories.

What I didn't realize until I had my first child was that nutrition is vital to the overall health equation. When my three-year-old son was diagnosed with late speech, the pediatrician suggested us to seek help. By chance, his pre-school teacher was piloting an after-school speech class in which he participated. After each class, as a reward, I would take him to McDonalds as it was right next door and my son was hungry. Thus, I would buy him either a small milkshake or happy meal three times a week. Not a big deal, I thought. Maybe a month or two into the program, he began having bad gastrointestinal problems; he wouldn't be able to control himself and would have a bowel movement in his pants. We were as frustrated as his teacher was. Therefore, I took him to the doctor because we were concerned about that turn of events. The pediatrician said he was lactose intolerant and we were told to give him pills and keep dairy away from him. Nevertheless, none of it worked and the problem continued. It affected playdates, school and likely his self-esteem.

A return trip to the doctor added no new information other than to continue the pills. During that time, I stopped buying him a milkshake at McDonalds, but continued purchasing other snacks there. Finally, it dawned on me that, after months of my son suffering from stomach issues, perhaps the fast food was the culprit. When I stopped all fast food, within a week, his stomach issues were resolved.

It was around that time that I realized how important food is on our body's overall health. My son and I watched *Super-Size Me*, the documentary on fast food, and it was so impactful that I began to change the way we ate.

I started noticing the effect it had on me not only physically but also mentally. When I ate more vegetables, organic healthy foods, I slept better; I felt better emotionally and I had more energy. My son had more energy too, and he no longer suffered any GI issues. They were gone!

I continued to explore ways to eat healthy while being a mom and working full-time. Eating healthy requires more money, more time for preparation and more creativity to make the food appealing.

In my 40s, I'm pretty aware of what fortifies my body and mind and what will detract from it. I have watched both of my boys eat poor quality, high fat foods; their bodies and attitudes suffer as a result. I am very clear that what goes into our bodies impacts our overall health and feeling of balance. I have seen the effect sugar has on my children; it was easier for me to see the result of sugar on their behavior and reactivity levels than seeing it in myself. However, as I became more aware of it in my children, I started noticing the significant effect sugar and saturated fatty foods played on my mental and emotional states. When I eat well, I feel well. When I omit sugar and fatty foods, I am calmer, I sleep better and I feel more clear-headed. Additionally, I am much better equipped to handle the stress of everyday life with less reactivity, and I no longer feel as though I am a victim of circumstances outside of my control.

Balance to me now means that my body is physically working in optimum condition. I sleep well (relatively speaking, since I have two dogs and two boys, so there is always something or someone that wakes me up at least once in the middle of the night), and I feel happy, enjoying many moments of peace and calm. When I get overwhelmed, which is easy for me having two boys in sports, a full time job in which I travel and being a single mom, I can verbalize my current state and find ways to take a time out.

And so, the secret recipe for balance? Balance is an ebb and flow, a relationship. It is not a destination; it is a journey. One I have had to work on moment by moment.

Many gurus recommend meditation and I agree. Meditation helps me to look inwards for peace instead of relying on a variety of outside distractions. I use the *Calm* app in the morning to do meditation, I journal, and I eat well, which means I eat foods that support the health of my body. I am finally at a point in my life where I do not shame myself often for eating a sweet treat; that is completely new experience for me!

What is the impact of what we eat? When we experience shame, guilt, sadness, or anger, it can ooze out onto family members, workmates, or both. Without the support to our bodies by eating well, exercising and using some form of meditation or journaling for self-discovery, we are more reactive. Stress adds fuel to the reactive equation as well, increasing cortisol levels and leading to a fight-or-flight mode. Therefore, physiologically, when we are stressed-out, our emotions are heightened and it is easier to fly off the handle. Stress, fast food, lack of sleep, no exercise—these are a recipe for disease to find its home in your body. It did in mine.

Some people are sensitive and feel the effects of stress on their bodies immediately; on the other hand, it may take a while in others. It can take the form of high blood pressure or high cholesterol. The pharmaceutical industry thrives because many of us go through life taking pills to solve our problems. Globally, it is estimated we will be spending $1.5 trillion on pharmaceutical drugs a year by 2021. We eat what is closest to us, we don't make time to exercise and we allow life to dictate how introspective we are or are not. Usually the latter.

I teach *Accountability* and I have been teaching it to individuals in organizations for years. They say when you teach something you learn to master it, and I am reminded daily that I have only started this journey. By working with people and organizations on this topic, I have increased my own self-awareness. And this self-awareness has saved my life.

After leaving the modeling scene, I finished my undergraduate degree and eventually my graduate degree. Then, I started in health care manufacturing in a sales role; that was my entrance into the corporate world. I stayed in the corporate world with various roles almost twenty years. Near the end of that part of my life, my colleague unexpectedly took his life. We had worked together for 10 years, so I was shocked by his abrupt ending and shocked at how my company handled it. I knew I was not long in that capacity; I wanted to do something to change the way people act in business. There was always this unwritten rule that you could not bring your personal side to work, which is extremely ridiculous. We are all people and we all come to work. We have stories, pain, joy and burdens that affect our whole being. We cannot separate these out and drop them off at day care until we return to pick them up again. Therefore, many of us mask that at work.

I left the same year Brian took his life, and within six

months, I was in a coaching certification program that changed the direction of my life. I had an opportunity to bring my genuine self to everything that I did and do. Shortly after, I joined Partners in Leadership, where I have been working with people in organizations to bring their true self to work through accountability. Accountability in a positive sense gives companies a competitive edge and creates a strong foundation in the business culture. I work across all industry, profit and non-profit organizations with teams and individuals.

While I coach both men and women, I have a passion for working with women in business. I am finishing a book focused on businesswomen owning their power and gracefully demonstrating their courage daily. This three-step process aligns our thinking and behaviors with our goals to achieve the outcomes we desire.

I speak to women's groups, I conduct webinars and I write for Forbes and Inc. I discovered that my purpose in life is to create a space for people to feel safe, to be real in both business and outside life as well. In doing so, they will own their value, their power and their voice. I do this through speaking events, writing, webinars, and any other venue I can create. I am passionate about my purpose.

Through my learnings, this journey has brought me to creating and hosting a forum for women to air their past, learn from others and find forgiveness. Through this process, we will heal our wounds. Stay tuned!

So, a few of my learnings from 49 years on this planet related to balance are:

• What we eat has a direct impact on our physical, mental and emotional state.

• If we have no physical activity in our lifestyle, this will affect our bodies negatively and will prevent us from having optimum health, including mental and emotional.

• Unprocessed experiences from childhood can leak out when we least expect it. Whether it might be poor body image or another unresolved issue, we have to deal with the skeletons in our closets.

• Negative chatter in our mind can be diluted with alternative approaches. Stuart Smalley had it right—positive affirmations help us to celebrate the goodness in ourselves. First and foremost, appreciation of self is healthy.

• Mindfulness is a choice, so incorporate some type of quiet time to process the day. This type of self-awareness is actually needed globally.

• Finally, balance is not something which will be achieved tomorrow at 4:30 P.M. It is a moment-by-moment recognition of my life and an opportunity to reassess. Am I balanced in this moment? And this one?

- Balance is a choice. Life sends curve balls to all of us, sometimes frequently, but we choose how we show up during these tough times.

How we treat our bodies, the foods we eat, the stress we allow to negatively affect us, and our emotional state will influence our chance of disease. However, we have a choice. Sometimes it doesn't feel like we do, but we choose how to respond to the people and situations in our life. We choose the food we eat, we choose how to care for our bodies and our mind, and we choose to emotionally overreact or take a breath and pause. The question is: do we prioritize self-love and compassion? Are those two at the bottom of our list, or do we make them part of our daily routine? Our decisions result in our effective or ineffective ability to cope with work and our relationships. Ultimately, that outcome influences those around us. So, when we feel stuck, like a victim, and we give in to that feeling, it will affect not only our state of being but that of those closest to us as well. We are all connected to one another on this planet, so the way we treat ourselves and others *matters*. We do have a choice.

Chapter 3

Unstoppable Success and the "UN-Do" List

Rhonda Kinard

No matter what people thought about me, said about me, or said to me, I always knew I would be an unstoppable success. Even when it appeared to the world, and to those closest to me, that my circumstances and my own massive mistakes were crushing me, I never once questioned the strength within me to survive, rise out of those moments, and achieve abundance, happiness, and success in life—my way, on my terms.

From growing into my womanhood, to making life choices that my family didn't always agree with or support, to finding my own voice and not being afraid to use it, to walking in purpose, to leaving corporate America, to becoming an entrepreneur and investor, to being unapologetically me, I've had to nurture my self-worth with the unwavering belief that my grand vision and the purpose positioned over my life were bigger, stronger, and more tenacious than any circumstance, roadblock, or detour I faced.

We all have the power within us to achieve unstoppable success in our lives because of the undeniable fire burning within each of us. Some of us are fanning that flame, while others are looking and searching everywhere for it, not knowing that it exists within them.

I'm here to shake your shoulders, disrupt your everyday patterns of thinking and living, and remind you that the only thing standing in the way of your unstoppable success is your inability to recognize the power and authority you have over your thoughts, actions, and progress. At any moment, you can decide that you are done playing small, playing it safe or watching from the sidelines, or not playing at all. In this world of "like me" and "follow me", we have been conditioned to think that it is other people's approval and opinions that matter most, and as such, we let others control our feelings, our possibilities, and our outcomes. We go looking for other people to show us the way, validate us, carry us safely and unscathed to our dream life and to the success we desire. However, the truth is, unstoppable success starts and ends with you.

When I decided to leave home, pursue a life with my then boyfriend (now husband of over seventeen years), and purchase my first house at the age of 21, I did not have my family's blessing. My parents eventually came around, but I had no emotional or financial support or access to the wisdom of my elders

45

who had been through the home buying process and who had also walked the path of a young woman just starting her life. I didn't wonder why no one supported me. I didn't question if people loved me. I never felt less of who I was even when others thought less of me, and I never gave the responsibility for my success to anyone else. My focus was on creating a life that I was proud of, that made me feel extremely good about who I was, and that allowed me to serve others from a full and grateful heart. It was the many moments like these that strengthened my will to make it. I am the woman I am today because every time my commitment to unstoppable success was tested, I persevered. I stayed focused, I passed, and I thrived.

Fast forward to now, I am an introverted mom, wife, entrepreneur, author, leader, and self-care fanatic with a fiery passion for inspiring, motivating and teaching others how to stand in their personal power, own their greatness and move through immeasurable odds and adversity to create the life they desire and deserve. It was this passion for serving others that led me to leave my six-figure career in the financial software and technology industry to pursue my big bodacious dreams of becoming a full-time personal power expert and learning and development professional. I am the founder of *A Life Ignited*, a company devoted to helping success-minded goal getters take their lives and careers from "great" to "next level extraordinary."

My coaching career started over 22 years ago when, as

a favor, I helped a friend prepare for an upcoming interview. Before our session together, my friend had gone on over ten interviews that all resulted in no job offers. I coached him on how to be confident and trust himself and his ability to be successful during his next interview. Two days after our session, he went on an interview that ended with a job offer right there on the spot. That was the beginning of my coaching career; I fell in love with helping people win and get what they want out of life. While working full time, raising small kids, and honing my real estate craft, I carved out time to take coaching classes and became a certified life coach, trainer, and speaker. Ultimately, *A Life Ignited, LLC* was born!

"A Life Ignited" is a state of mind; a lifestyle rooted and fueled by the belief that you are an unstoppable success in your own right. Your success, your next best season and most extraordinary level takes flight when you first clean off and clear all the debris from your runway. Wheels up! It's time to break free from habits, attitudes, and crowds that compromise your unstoppable success.

Are you ready to soar? The most mind-blowing, top of the world, wildly successful, and soul-fulfilling moments of your life are not the result of the things that you "do"; they are the reward and fruit from the behaviors, patterns, and limiting mindsets that you "undo" on your journey.

"Create the highest, grandest vision possible for your life, because you become what you believe"

– Oprah Winfrey

Taking your life to the next level requires you to break out and let go of people, places, and things that no longer serve you. The struggle for many visionary purpose-driven women (and men) who are not walking in the fullness of who they've been called to be is not that they are without a grand vision of their lives. It's not even that they don't believe they can achieve their goals and create a life that sets their soul on fire. Most of us, success-minded types, are taking action and standing in our power as best we can; however, even with all our efforts and hard work, there is still a disconnect between where we are now and where we know we should be. And that disconnect, that gap, is the result of trying to move forward toward your most incredible life while still carrying on with the same thinking, thoughts, and toxic things you were attached to before you decided to pursue your purpose, passion, and divine assignment.

Let me break that down a bit further. The reason you have not achieved the levels of happiness, peace of mind, fulfillment, and success (mind, body, and spirit) you desire is that there are some goal-adverse behaviors in your daily habits and patterns of living that you have not committed to "un"doing. Until you stop dragging around that dead weight, you'll find yourself exhausted and frustrated with no results.

It wasn't until I took an honest look at my daily patterns, who I talked to, how I spent my time, who I spent my time with, and the self-sabotaging things I would tell myself, that I began to experience transformation in a real way. I contribute my achievements and sustained successes with my health, body and fitness, entrepreneurial endeavors, and relationships to the creation and my unapologetic commitment to an un-do list.

I created my first un-do list in the fall of 2016. I realized towards the end of that year that while I had given so much energy, effort, and financial resources to my personal development and growth, I was still considerably far from where I wanted to be. I began to ask myself, "What are you doing that is standing in the way of who you desire to be and what you desire to have?"

For so long, I focused on the behaviors and strategies I needed to add to my life, but what I never considered was what I needed to stop doing to stand fully in my personal power and create the magic I so desperately desired and knew I was capable of achieving. I realized the missing link was a soulful deep dive into what I needed to "undo".

One Sunday afternoon, I walked into my home office, grabbed a journal and some colored pens and stickers, and I created my very first "Un-Do" list. I still have that list today. On the first blank page of the journal, in big bold letters across the top, I wrote "Un-Do" *List*. Under that, I wrote the words,

"Things I want to stop doing." From there I began to compile a list of things I knew were distracting and disrupting my progress on my goals. The moment my un-do list was born, my breakthrough was ignited and all the possibilities for my life were unleashed.

What I know for certain is that once you begin to examine your life with humble and honest eyes, it will become clear to you that there are some actions, mindsets, and people that you are pulling along with you that are both incapable and unqualified to travel with you to your next best level of life and business.

This isn't theory. I'm speaking to you from experience, and these are lessons I had to learn the hard way. I know what it's like to work consistently at something, put your whole self into it and then not see any results. I know how frustrating it can be when you see everyone else doing what you want to do, or enjoying the very things you want to enjoy, yet what's real and attainable for others seems impossible and out of reach for you. There was a time I worked extremely hard to lose weight, get my body back in shape, create a less hectic and disorganized lifestyle, and get healthy so I could defeat the chronic medical conditions that resulted from my poor dietary choices and lack of self-care. I can remember days where I felt defeated and crushed because I didn't understand why I was going to the gym, eating more greens and veggies, and taking the stairs at work, but not seeing the changes in my blood pressure readings or on the scale. At that time, my blood pressure was dangerously high. On one awful occasion, I suffered partial blindness in my right eye from a condition known as hypertension retinopathy.

I envied women who I followed on Facebook who were able to quit their jobs, transition into second careers, and make a profit working full time in their passion. For a long time, I wondered what was so special about them and why they seemed to have the secret formula to success that I didn't have.

Today, I am in the best physical shape of my entire life, I am successfully managing my blood pressure, and I no longer look at other women with envious eyes or a sullen spirit because now I'm living in my purpose, working in my gifts, and living the life I dreamed about—my way, on my terms. And I owe these successes, in part, to my "Un-Do" list.

As you step into your personal power and begin to make the transformational lifestyle changes required for your next level, you will need to create and get to work on an "Un-Do" list of your own. An un-do list is not optional—it's a requirement for attaining the levels of fulfillment and success you crave.

You have been called to greatness. Abundance is your birthright! You have the power within you to fulfill every desire of your heart. The gift of unstoppable success has your name on it, but until you let go of some of that toxic guck in your life, you will always struggle to unwrap it.

Now, let's talk about your "Un-Do" list.

As busy purpose-driven men and women, many of us rely on a to-do list to help us stay on track with our responsibilities. However, the un-do list serves a different purpose; an un-do list is an empowerment tool for growth and goals achieved. One of the reasons I was frustrated with my chronic illnesses and weight gain was because while I had a to-do list of healthy habits and activities to add to my day, I did not consider the behaviors and habits I needed to undo to achieve the success I was seeking. Yes, I was eating more greens, veggies, and bananas: That was all on my to-do list. Yes, I started going to the gym more often—that was on my to-do list. Yes, I started drinking more water—that was on my to-do list as well. I was doing all these tremendously heart-healthy things, but still having no success with my wellness goals.

Do you feel like you're doing everything you're supposed to do, yet you are not having the success you expect? I invite you to consider that the reason you are not having the success you expect is that while you have incorporated productive actions into your routine, you still have counter-productive behaviors in your life that neutralize and fizzle the strength and trans-formational power of the good new habits. This is where the un-do list will change your life. While my to-do list said to drink more water, I had an un-do list action item to stop drinking so much soda. Where my to-do list called for me to eat more greens and vegetables, my un-do list instructed me to stop eating frozen dinners for lunch. My grand vision called for me to step out on faith and start my own training and coaching company, and for the company to be successful, my un-do list called for me to strip away my fear of failure.

My challenge for you, at this very moment in your life, is to commit yourself to create an un-do list. Your un-do list should answer one fundamental question... What is the thing that I continually do that consistently keeps me from being connected and fully committed to who I desire to be, who I've been called to serve, and how I want to feel?

I want you to stop for a moment and think about something you desire to have that you have wanted for a very long time, something you've struggled to achieve or access. Whether it is a health and wellness milestone, a relationship goal, a career goal, or a project, I want you to think about that thing you desire so badly. Then, ask yourself again... What is the thing that I continually do that consistently keeps me from being connected and fully committed to who I desire to be, who I've been called to serve, and how I want to feel?

Then, without judging yourself, answer it truthfully. The answer to that question is now the first "undo" action on your new un-do list.

Do you remember my first un-do list, the one I created

in the fall of 2016? Well, my very first un-do action was "Using social media or the internet as a vehicle for laziness or procrastination."

I don't know what your first "un-do" action is, but in this moment of authenticity and self-awareness, you have revealed one of the things you need to undo or give up in your life to achieve the results you desire.

The goal of the un-do list is not to bring you down or make you feel negative about yourself; on the contrary, it is meant to light your path and guide your transformation. The un-do list is a beautiful thing. It's honest, authentic, delivered 'by you for you' from a deep and heart-centered place within, that wants to see you feel good, do good, and succeed in life.

The un-do list is a transferable tool that you can use not only in your personal life, but it's also a tool you can use to facilitate growth and development, build better teams, improve your influence and leadership at work, and cultivate better relationships.

Can you see the value of having an un-do list in your life? The coach in me cannot bring our time together to a close without first ensuring that you are set up to use your new un-do list in a powerful and productive way. That is why I'm giving you an *ignited* Action Item right now. Yes, you have homework. Surprise!

Your homework is to continue creating your "Un-Do" List.

If you're creative like me, grab the colored pens and pencils, the stickers, embellishments, and a blank piece of paper and start to design your un-do list. If you're thinking, "Ain't nobody got time for all of that!" then ditch the colored pens and stickers. You can also create a Google doc or use some sort of notes app on your phone to create your list.

To get you started, I am going to give you four actions to put on your un-do list. While I don't know you personally, what I do know from my years as a certified life coach, personal power expert, mom, wife, and big bodacious goal-getter myself, is that all visionary goal-centric women (and men) struggle with many of the same mindset hurdles and setbacks. By adding a few of the most common actions that hold us back to your un-do list now, I'll know that you're on the right track, and that you have actions you can begin to take immediately to transform your mindset and your life.

Add these four things to your un-do list:

#1. Making excuses and saying what you can't do or what you don't have time for.

I was eight months pregnant, sitting in a real estate class for three hours in the evenings after working full time as a software professional. I was tired, swollen, and, most nights, miserable, but I wanted to become a licensed real estate agent, and that meant being uncomfortable, trading my excuses for execution, and making things happen. The grand vision for my life included owning investment properties and becoming knowledgeable about the real estate industry. By any means necessary, pregnant and all, I had to do the uncomfortable work and take inconvenient action to achieve my goals and live my dreams. The dream wasn't about me, it was about the children I would soon birth; it was about giving them the financial foundation in life that I didn't have when I was growing up. No excuse was more significant than my desire to provide for my unborn children.

I had to make the time to take my real estate courses. I had to find time in my hectic schedule to write my book. I had to become the artistic and creative director of my life, so I could pull off working a full-time job while working on my passion and in my new business part time. I didn't have time for "I can't", "It's too hard," or "I don't have time." And neither do you!

From now on, every time you start a sentence with "I can't" or "I don't have the time to," I want you to reframe that sentence and say, "My dreams are bigger than my excuses, and I do have the time to_____." Focused on your grand vision and the divine calling on your life, complete the sentence.

#2. Looking for validation from people who cannot validate you.

How many times have wanted someone, whose opinion you really value, to be excited about your grand vision and big goals, and when they weren't excited and looked at you like you had two heads, you gave up on your dream and stopped working towards it?

Today is the day you stop letting people and their opinions and insecurities keep you stuck, scared, and afraid. No one can validate what has already been divinely mandated over your life. It is your time to soar. It is your time to shine. It is your time to serve the world with your talent, gifts, and enthusiasm. You have been given priority boarding to take flight and thrive. Why would you give up that privilege, your first-class status, and your purposeful assignment because someone else doesn't believe in the power within you to create something beautiful and extraordinary? People who haven't tapped into their fullest potential will never understand why you have unapologetically tapped into yours. And that's okay, it's perfectly fine that they just don't get it!

Nevertheless, don't expect people to your see vision, and don't punish them because they don't see it. You are the only one in the world with the optic ability to see the greatness that has been positioned over your life. Validation has been given. Access has already been granted. Now, it's time for you to go, sow, and be great.

#3. Thinking you need something else.

You don't need a fancy website. You don't need thousands

of followers. You don't even need to kiss anybody's derrière because you think they're the link in the chain that will connect you to all the people you think you need to know. All you need to do is be committed and connected to your next best level and who you've been called to serve.

When I started my coaching and training business *A Life Ignited*, I was still working full time for a financial software company. I did not have a lot of money or time to spend on marketing. I waited for Vistaprint to have one of their 50% off sales to order the cheapest business cards they sold. I asked a Facebook friend to create a postcard graphic for me, and I ordered 50 postcards that I mailed to various learning institutions around Philadelphia. Of the 25 postcards I sent out in that first batch, one very prominent organization called me for an interview and ultimately contracted with me for one year. It wasn't fancy marketing or professional pictures that sealed the deal—it was my passion for my purpose that got me noticed and booked.

Your purpose will take you to the places you need to go. Your purpose will bring the people that want your product, service, talents, and gifts to you. You don't need to chase people. You don't need to spend all your money on gadgets, tools, and software. Use what you have and start where you are. Let your purpose and grand vision be the seeds. Start planting now.

#4. Talking yourself into inaction.

Have you ever had an idea that you thought was amazing and you knew would be successful, but as you started thinking about all the moving parts and things that need to happen to make that idea a reality, you overwhelmed yourself and talked yourself into doing nothing and taking no action?

Take each moment of your big vision as it comes. For now, focus on the first step. Don't get worked up and scared thinking about the seventeenth step. By the time you get to the seventeenth step, steps one through sixteen will have already prepared you for what it will take to conquer step seventeen. When you get to each new level, you will be prepared and ready.

As you take each step and move to each new level, refer to your un-do list and determine what you need to undo so you can achieve the results you desire. Ask yourself... What baggage (mind, body, and spirit) do I need to let go of to take this next step successfully? Once you have those answers, begin the necessary work of undoing everything that's keeping you from creating, living, and fully experiencing all that you desire and deserve.

You, beautiful visionary woman (or man) of purpose, make it a priority to create and build out your "Un-Do" list. If you are ready to take your life to the next level, lead with excellence, serve with a grateful heart, and unlock the best, brightest, and most brilliant parts of yourself, you must first breakaway, let go, and free yourself from everything and anybody that is holding you back.

Let your un-do list power your passion for service, ignite next level excellence in all that you pursue, and fuel your unstoppable success.

Be Motivated. Be Inspired. Be A Life Ignited.

xx, Coach Rhonda.

Chapter 4

"Mental Health" is NOT a Dirty word. Are you doing what is needed to create a good mental health environment as a Leader?

Maggie Georgopoulos

Whether you are a leader who, at some stage, may suffer from mental health issues, or one of the few who have never experienced a period of poor mental health, it is important to create an environment that's friendly toward those who may be dealing with mental health issues regardless of whether these are short or long term.

One of the biggest workplace problems is stress. Stress is not a mental health condition; however, it does have the potential to contribute to a mental health condition if it is at a high level over a prolonged period of time. This can be caused by working conditions, how people treat you, or even your own perceptions of what you should be doing. Women, in their effort to be "superwomen" and fit to a perception of what modern

61

society wants from them, tend to be more affected than men.

In the United Kingdom, according to the National Health Service, 1 in 4 women will have depression as opposed to 1 in 10 men. Additionally, in the UK 29% of women report a major mental health issue compared to 17% of men. Women are twice as likely as men to experience some kind of anxiety disorder. According to the Australian Bureau of Statistics, 22% of women are likely to experience a mental health issue for 12 months or more as compared to 17% of men. Moreover, in the United States, a study reported in Time Magazine showed 9% of women and 5% of men had experienced depression in the previous 12 months, with 23% of women having an anxiety disorder compared with 14% of men.

If we look at it from a global perspective, a World Health Organisation report also shows women are more likely to be affected by mental health issues. The latest statistics, as summarised in a report for the 2013 - 2020 Mental Health Action Plan, are:

• Depressive disorders account for close to 41.9% of disability from neuropsychiatric disorders among women compared to 29.3% among men.

• Leading mental health problems in older adults are depression, organic brain syndromes and dementia—the majority of those with the disorders are women.

- An estimated 80% of 50 million people affected by violent conflicts, civil wars, disasters, and displacement are women and children.

- Lifetime prevalence rate of violence against women ranges from 16% to 50%.

- At least one in five women suffer rape or attempted rape in their lifetime.

These last three statistics are important, as they highlight why it is that women have a higher prevalence of mental health conditions than men. It is it not genetics, but rather, our environmental factors.

Mental health has a major impact on the workplace and in our businesses whether we like it or not. As a result of the stigma around mental health, staff are lost and there is a reduction of trust and a higher possibility of workplace stress. Whilst mental health is now talked about, and at last, even governments are trying to make a difference, it is going to take a much greater effort to eliminate this stigma. It is costing businesses worldwide approximately US$1450 per year per employee in lost time due to mental health conditions at the time of writing this.

As a leader, you have a responsibility to create an environment where people feel comfortable and are happy to speak to you about their issues. This can be difficult in a workplace where so little is understood about mental illness and how it can, and does, affect our ability to communicate and work.

Before we go much further into the steps to create a mental health friendly business or work environment as a leader, I will share why it is something I focus so closely on, in my writing, podcasts and interviews around the world...

I am bipolar. My Cyclothymic Bipolar disorder does not affect my day-to-day ability to work, in fact, a lot of the time it has enabled me to achieve some good things rather than spoil them. Even in my depressive episodes, I have been able to achieve. Unfortunately, due to the actions of one person when, at the age of seventeen, I revealed my disorder, I subsequently decided it was better to keep such information to myself. Thus, it has taken me nearly 30 years to open up and tell even those who are closest to me about it. To the extent that my best friend, who herself has experienced poor mental health from time to time, only found out about it when she proofread a chapter I wrote in my book!

At seventeen, I opened up and told teachers at my school what was happening to me. Most were sympathetic, supportive and eager to do what they could to help. Unfortunately, one was less sympathetic and, breaching confidentiality, relayed something I had told them in confidence to other students. If this was not enough, he took it upon himself to inform everyone I was crazy and blaming staff for my problems! This was extremely unprofessional and left me feeling I was to blame for revealing how I felt. Possibly because of his attitude, which might well have affected my ambition, I worked extremely hard and was awarded the Science Dux without the help of my unsupportive chemistry teacher.

By the time I was thirty-two, times had changed a little, but as I was working in an all-male environment and had just been appointed chair of the board, I felt this was not the time to reveal anything that might indicate I was weak in any way. So, not only did I deal with this in private, revealing my depression only to close family, but I managed to keep my suicidal turn from the business as well.

None of what I have revealed is, in any way, to suggest I am amazing or to highlight the need for support and understanding. As a leader with a mental health disorder, that I deal with on a daily basis, I am more attuned to the need to be open and approachable, which must have communicated itself to others in the way I operate, as I have always the been the recipient of my team's confidences.

Sadly, over the years, I have seen far too many leaders who consider that the "go home and get over it" mantra is appropriate. I particularly remember that supervisor who told me to "go home, get some sleep, and come back in the morning ready to work!" in a not so positive light. To make matter worse this organisation prided it on being supportive of their staff's mental health!

Cognitive Bias and mental health

Recently, understanding cognitive biases as leaders has become a thing that many businesses have started working towards training their staff in. This is a key area for diversity and inclusion, whether it is around gender, sexuality, race, religion, colour, or a list of many other things we are trying to prove we are diverse by talking about.

What is cognitive bias? We all have biases whether we realise it or not, the thing is most of them are unconscious. This occurs because of how our brains function. To make it a

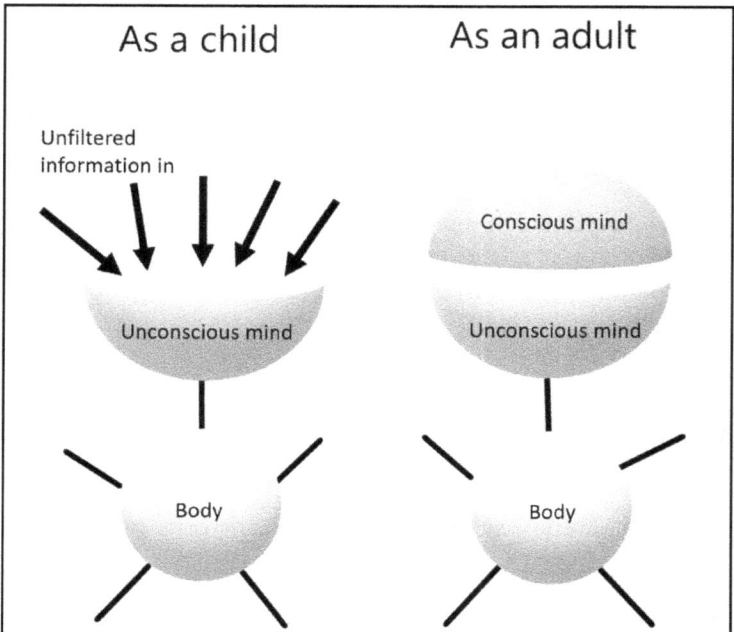

As a child | As an adult

Unfiltered information in

Conscious mind

Unconscious mind | Unconscious mind

Body | Body

little easier to understand, I want you to look at some brain science and I will distil it into simple, easy to understand terms. Mainly because that is how I like to work with things, it makes it easier for me to understand it.

When we are children, our brain is essentially a sponge. Everything we experience just drops into it unfiltered. For example, we come home one day from school with a picture of our family that we have lovingly created. You know, the one with the house that is the same size as the family members and often the people don't really look like people. We excitedly show the picture to our parents and they lovingly praise the picture, discuss it with us and then put it up on the fridge for everyone to see. The unfiltered message that drops into our heads is that we are good at art and our parents like it when we are creative (or something similar). If, however, we get a "that's nice, sweetie" and the picture is absentmindedly put aside, then the unfiltered message is likely to be something like, "I wasn't good enough," or "I can't draw or paint."

This is just one example, and I don't use it to try to highlight good or bad parents. We all have absentminded or distracted days and we all react to things differently. This doesn't make us good or bad, it's just how it is. I use it to illustrate what happens.

Up to the age of six or seven, we continue to take unfiltered information, and this information forms a part of our unconscious. As we continue to grow, we now filter some things, but many others are still dropping in unfiltered. All of this information forms our unconscious and builds our personal biases.

As adults, we now have filters in place—Conscious and Unconscious. The unconscious filters will take information and only pay attention to the information that matches the bias we have developed through our developing years. As it is unconscious, it takes a bit of work to notice our own way of reacting to things in order for us to make it a conscious bias and then change it.

What does this look like?

There is a gender bias exercise called the surgeon story. It goes like this:

A man and a boy are in a car accident. The man dies at the scene. The boy is taken to hospital. The surgeon, about to operate, looks at the boy and says, "I can't operate on this boy, he is my son."

Who is the surgeon?

I have conducted this many times in training to demonstrate unconscious bias and the results are awesome. If you haven't done it before, try to work it out before reading on.

Among many answers, the most popular are that the surgeon is the boy's biological father, it is a gay couple, and that the man in the accident wasn't the boy's father. I have even seen a survey conducted in the streets by the BBC in which people have said it was a priest or even god!

The surgeon is the boy's mother. Only about 5 – 10% of us will get it, though that may be changing the more this particular exercise is done, even when it is a room full of women. This happens because when we were at school all the pictures we saw of doctors or surgeons were male. Think about it with other roles as well. Nurses and teachers were women, police and construction workers were men and so on.

If this is the case with gender, imagine what has happened with our unconscious biases and mental health. Over the years, we have been taught not to speak about it and we see media coverage only showing the negative aspects of mental health conditions. As such we associate mental health with negative things, including the idea that if someone has depression, anxiety or any other mental health condition they are not able to work.

Mental Health in the workplace

The first thing I want to make clear here is we all have mental health, just as we all have physical health. It can be good, bad, or anything in between. The clear difference between our mental health and most physical health conditions is that it cannot be seen and shows up differently in different people. Anxiety in one person is not the same as anxiety in the next because we don't have the same triggers.

On my leadership journey, with bipolar disorder, I have had many bumps in the road and a pothole or two. One of the hardest parts in my climb was keeping my mental health condition to myself; my experience at an early age made me feel that if I told people about it, I would be ridiculed and treated differently. In the many phases of my journey, it wasn't until I was running my own business that I felt comfortable coming out to the world about my mental health. Part of the reason was the environments I worked and studied in.

I had decided to undertake a degree in Mechanical Engineering. That decision had come about due to time I spent working at the BHP Steelworks as an apprentice electrician (seeing a bit of trend with what I like to do?). I really loved working in the areas with the heavy machinery and I also had the advantage of befriending the mature apprentices. These were men who had already worked for at least 10 years within the organisation and where training for a trade. They showed me that being a woman was enough of a disadvantage without sharing my mental health condition with anyone and helped me to appreciate the machinery even more.

At university, I was faced with yet another culture of male dominance and being at a disadvantage as a woman. Even though I had earned my place in the degree, I was unfortunate to start in a year that the University had started a program that tried to get more women into Engineering. They removed the need for Physics and for the higher-level maths for 150 students. These groups were actually a mix of male and female, but I and the other seven females among the other 400 students who had all the subjects and marks required, we were constantly being told we only got in because of our gender. The worst part was that many of the "boys" who made that judgement didn't even do as well as we did!

It was yet another early experience for me regarding the way culture can affect the decisions we make and what we are willing to share. In order to compensate and gain back control, I stepped into one of my first leadership roles and became the president of the Young Engineers Club. The largest club on campus and the one with the least number of females as members.

As leaders, we need to be the ones that step forward to help change the dynamic around mental health in the workplace. As this is a cultural change, it is not something that can be done over night, or just by us. We can set an example in how we look after our staff and ourselves.

Culture in an organisation is the sum total of the values, biases and actions of the individuals that make up the organisation. This means that we cannot just create a few posters, put a memo and then have it changed. It will not happen over night. Remember; we have hundreds of years of being told that poor mental health is a bad thing, that people with mental health conditions can't function in the real world, and that you can't work if you have a mental health condition.

Scarily, we were still blaming many mental health conditions on women as recently as the 1930s, hence the word hysteria (meaning madness of the womb). It was only in the 1970s and 1980s, when I was growing up, that we were moving from institutionalising people for any mental health condition and looking at alternative ways of treating it.

I repeat myself—Trying to change the perception of how it is going to be received and treated in an organisation is not going to happen overnight.

Leading a mental health supportive environment

As a leader, there are things that you can do in order to change this issue. It starts with small things, such as ensuring that people are aware of what your organisations practices around mental health are. Is counselling offered? Are there support groups? How are management and human resources involved in the process? Are there independent Mental Health First aiders in your workplace?

One way to ensure your team knows you are supportive is talking about mental health. Have regular team meetings where you might have a five or ten minute taster session on an aspect of mental health and then looking after it.

Another thing that is important to do as a leader is to make sure your team knows that you are someone approachable and that, unlike my chemistry teacher, you are able to keep the information confidential. One way to do this is to make it a part of the monthly one-to-one sessions you have with your staff in order to chat about how things are going. This is not a work review session but rather a session where you sit with a cup of coffee and just talk about what is working and what isn't at home or at work, at a level they are comfortable with. Remember, getting to know your team is an important aspect of being a good leader.

I encourage leaders to not to be as I was. Whilst in all my roles in leadership, from those first steps I have discussed at university, all the way through to when I stepped into the role as the Executive Chairman of the Board of a large Agricultural Company in Australia, I kept my bipolar disorder to myself. This is not healthy nor does it help to cultivate a culture of trust. As I mentioned earlier in the chapter, I took a path of stepping into leadership roles almost as a way to compensate for the many perceived disadvantages I had (being a woman, having a mental health condition, and being of mixed race origin). I stepped out of University into a well-paying Engineering role at Toyota Australia; this came about because, in order to fund my way through my degree, I had managed to graduate with

4 years of work experience as an engineer. Not bad for one of the two women who graduated in my year... but that is for another story.

I was someone that people would feel comfortable talking to about their health, both mental and physical, or any other issues they had. I unfortunately had an iron cage around my own "secrets". I was still young when I reached the top of my ladder, only 32; I was still inexperienced. The one thing I was very experienced at was complying with what society dictates on people with mental health conditions; by not talking about it. You see, it was still very much a time of mental health being a taboo topic.

On reflection, I see that I was accidently approachable because my barriers were also a barrier to me being able to lead well, and they were also a barrier to me properly managing my condition. By keeping secrets, I was not taking care of my mental health.

Taking care of your mental health

As both a leader and an individual, you owe it to yourself to look after your greatest asset—your health, both mental and physical. You would go to the doctor if you had flu or some other physical illness, and in the same way, you need to make sure you receive the right advice and attention when there are problems with your mental health.

Many people can be "cured". Just as we will have a physical complaint at times, many of us will end up with depression, stress related illnesses, or anxiety, which will be brought on by a particular set of circumstances. Often, once these circumstances are removed, dealt with in some other way, or a sufficient amount of time has elapsed since they occurred, we will recover.

When the problem is an inherent part of who you are, it also needs to be looked after. We need to ensure we have counselling if it works; take the pills if that is what you need to do to reduce the intensity of an anxiety attack; or look at our current situation and find ways to cope with it so we can continue working. This is not about giving up dreams; this is about looking after yourself, so you can experience the maximum success possible.

Key steps you can take to ensure your mental health:

#1. Talk about your feelings.

This does not mean talking to all and sundry about them. Talk to people you trust and who will understand your needs, but not necessarily feel the need to "fix you".

#2. Keep active.

Whilst this is difficult, particularly when you are crippled with an anxiety attack or in the midst of a depressive episode, it is a good habit to maintain. It really does help your mental health to be active.

#3. Ask for help.

If you are feeling overwhelmed in some way, or even if it has not yet reached this stage, it is sensible to ask for help.

#4. Don't forget to take time for yourself.

Take a break. It could be reading a book or watching your favourite TV show without feeling guilty. It could be a spa day, a short break holiday, or walking in the hills. Whatever it is you do to relax, remember to timetable it into your life, especially when you are busy.

I have experience firsthand what happens when you don't take care of your mental health. Regardless of if you end up diagnosed with something that is more "short-term", or have a condition like the one I have, which is a part of you and needs to be managed for the rest of your life (much like type one diabetes, for example), you need to take care of it. If you don't, you end up making things worse.

During my time as Executive Chairman of the Board, my bipolar was running unchecked. I was not medicated, and I ignored what was triggering episodes of manic highs or lows. In some ways, I achieved much because of the highs, but I also risked my life. This is neither logical nor sensible. I also became very adept at fooling my counsellors, so I didn't have to spend time talking to them. I was not looking after myself.

During that time, two key incidents happened that opened my eyes up and made me stop and take a long hard look at my life. The first one was my third attempt at suicide. I had been in my position for about 6 months at the time and was riding a manic high. The problem was that I lose track of time when I am on a high and I flattened out the day before the company broke up for the Easter break. In many states in Australia, you will often end up with five days off for this break and that is exactly what happened to us. As I was leaving work for the start of the break, I realised that I was going to be alone for the next five days and it dropped me into a manic-depressive episode (yes, it can be that quick to cause a change of mood).

Not a single person in the workplace would ever find out about my attempt to end my life or the fact that my life was saved by seeking out an ex-boyfriend and crashing his quiet time.

The second thing that happened was my physical health deteriorated. I woke up one morning at 2 a.m. and was haemorrhaging. My body had rebelled against the long hours, lack of sleep and, more importantly, very poor diet. I can no longer eat gluten because of the way I treated my body; I turned a mild intolerance into a serious allergy.

At this point, I realised that I had to stop ignoring the signs my mind and body were giving out and look after myself. That was the point I started managing my bipolar disorder better. I paid attention to my triggers and whilst I may not be able to stop a manic high or low, I can prepare for it, as I know it is coming. I can also manage things to avoid triggers when possible. This is the point I decided to step off the ladder, look at my whole life, and decide if it was what I really wanted to do.

Leading is but working in the corporate world, and living a lie isn't what I want in my life. Which is how I came to be running my own company.

What do you need to look at in your life which may be leading to poor health?

Another little exercise I like to get people to do is to take the time to sit down on a regular basis and take an inventory of those whom you can speak to about your mental health. I have found from experience, both my own and that of those I have worked with over the years, that when we are in the middle of a period of poor mental health, it is hard to think clearly. This means that we will come up with excuses and reasons why people don't want to talk with us.

I have found that if you sit down for about five or so minute once a month and list people you can speak to, then this helps when you need it most. This is as the list will be in the forefront of your mind.

Exercise:

List (approximately five but at least one) people in your everyday life you can speak to about your mental health.

```

```

List (approximately three but at least one) people in your business or workplace you can

```

```

List (approximately five but at least one) people in your business or workplace you can speak to about your mental health

```

```

As leaders, this is something you can ask your team members to do. Remember, this list is only for the person writing it.

If you get your team members to do it, make it clear that they are doing this just for themselves and you don't want to see who is on their lists.

It is important as leaders to be aware of how mental health can affect both yourself and your team. It doesn't matter what your gender is. If you are to be a true leader, you need to consider your mental health and what needs to be done to support it. Take steps today to make sure you are looking after your mental health and your team's.

Chapter 5

Always Look Up

Leslie Thomas Flowers

As a young girl growing up outside of Boston, down Route 9, in a little town called Natick, I lived a charmed life. I was a ballet dancer at the Boston Conservatory of Music, later I was a high school student and subsequently a college student at San Francisco State, and then I served as a flight attendant taking troops in and out of Vietnam during the war. I was a free spirit and was full of myself; I loved living in San Francisco, dancing Flamenco and driving around in my 1960 TR3.

I married on June 6, 1968 on a whim. I was studying flamenco dance and my boyfriend played the guitar. We ran off to Reno on the same day Bobby Kennedy was assassinated; however, it was over in eighteen months. We drove as newlyweds to New York and lived about twenty blocks from my paternal grandmother, who had lived there most of her adult life and would walk the long blocks when I got sick, carrying homemade chicken soup.

Not too long, when *he* didn't come home one night after

Woodstock, the writing was on the wall and I hopped on a plane back to the Bay Area. It was too much, and I wanted to go home. So, I did it.

I married for the second time in 1972 to a southern guy my age (we were both born in 1946); we both worked at Blythe & Company in San Francisco. Then, we moved to North Carolina, had our ups and downs, yet all in all with our two healthy beautiful children and a home in the woods that we loved. Life was good for thirty years.

At the turn of this century, however, I found myself sitting alone in the dark for two years in the home I loved so much, where had I raised my two children over two decades. Overnight, it became my tomb, a place to give up and die, and I wore an imaginary and constant dark veil that let in no light. I went to work every day, came home, and cried. One day my thirty-year marriage was alive; the next it was dead—dead as a doornail.

What happened "overnight" was the devastation and end of the life I had been living happily for as long as I could remember. This was the implosion of my own *American dream* right before my eyes. When I walked through the house, it felt like I was walking over earthquake rubble—with no sure footing, as it felt my roots had been cut right down to the quick.

I did some crazy things, things that when I try look at now,

I'd rather not look at all, to "stop the change that was inevitable." My *American dream* of a marriage was about never giving up. I was proud we had made it thirty years in the face of divorce now being the norm. That meant sticking with it no matter what. It meant keeping my word; the word I had given before God, family and friends. It meant doing "whatever it took" to maintain that family unit. Eventually, however, the writing was on the wall. I treated myself to a long running love affair with a French-Canadian filmmaker. I deserved it.

I was 55. Both children were on their own. All retirement money to the tune of about $700,000 and property vanished into what seemed like thin air, almost overnight. While I was working and "healing," my husband and I lived in different domiciles. He had been "investing" all our life savings without my knowledge. The investments yielded a big fat goose egg and I walked away after thirty years with $4,000 in my pocket. Eventually, I picked myself up by the bootstraps and began living life again. The veil almost never showed up now as a reminder… and life was getting good again.

Coming home from work one Friday afternoon, I grabbed the mail and looked at it in the car. There was a letter from the IRS. I opened it and what I read threw me for a loop. The instructions after *Dear Mrs. Flowers* were to include my first monthly payment of $5,000 to pay back $80,000 I owed the Federal government!

I was a secretary with a net income of about $3,000 a month at that time. There was no way! How did this happen?

The way I saw it, I had three choices. One was to throw in the towel and sell everything, living on the street and trudging with the homeless. Second was to let them take me to jail. And third was drive off a bridge.

That was wrong. I knew that wasn't my doing, yet does it matter who is responsible when it comes to owing and having a face-off with the government?

Then I remembered I had $500 stashed away in an Edward Jones account and I knew the broker well. I called him, went in the next day, and told him what happened. What he said changed the course of my life. I didn't know it then because I had simply sought "specialized knowledge" (expert advice), which I learned later in my studies is a critical element in applying the principles of success for achievement—in business and in life. He told me I needed a tax attorney who is also a CPA, and he had a recommendation.

Eighteen months later and $5,000 to the attorney, $50,000 of the $80,000 was removed from my debt. I was quiet when the attorney told me we had done well, he asked inside a very uncomfortable "pregnant" pause, if I wanted to appeal. Yes, I said. Twelve months and $1,800 later, the entire $80k was removed from my debt.

My credit was in the toilet of course, but I was coming out of that too.

This woman lived a colorful life. College in San Francisco, flight attendant shuttling US troops into and out of Vietnam in the 60s (with overnights in Hawaii, Philippines and Japan), danced Flamenco, studied humanities at San Francisco State, performed for Burt Lancaster at UCLA her junior year in high school, was in a folk group, and played in a rock band. Nothing ever stopped me. I was always moving forward. The Universe always had a wind at my back.

One day after picking up the mail, I saw a letter from the State department of revenue. "*Dear Mrs. Flowers*… you owe us $20,000. And here is your payment book, etc., etc…" Really? When I shared my saga with the State staff member in charge, they waived that $20,000 as well, so I was debt free! Well, not exactly.

I wrote my 2014 Amazon bestseller Champion as the unofficial *Think and Grow Rich for Women* so that whoever read it would have easy access to understanding to never give up no matter how tough your plight may seem.

Over dinner one night with some of my mastermind clients, I got the idea to write that book; I excused myself from the table, ran to the computer and bought all three web sites for ten dollars each. The sites were to be mine… The universe wanted it for me and held them for me; I was sure.

I have to say my book is *unofficial* as I ran into the Napoleon Hill Foundation and they "sicked" a women attorney after me to stop me from writing and to get the three web sites back, *or else*! Daily emails and phone calls from her went on for weeks telling me that I couldn't write the book and what they would do if I didn't turn over those sites. Note: make your sites private so no one knows who owns them.

A friend and IP attorney did a little digging only to find out that the foundation not only spent funds going after me for weeks, they also added to the trademark that I could never write the book. Were they really afraid of a retired grandmother?

How did they find out I was writing it? Good question. I went to my mentor Bob Proctor with the book to get his guidance. I had invested some $2,100 in his training and buying his business in a box, so I thought he was my mentor. The lesson—teachers are not necessarily our mentors. My next step was to go to the Foundation, of course.

I never spoke to Proctor, but passed the information and my book outline to his assistant and within two days the Foundation gorillas were at my door. Even now, sharing this, I am afraid they will come after me again with their big guns and money. All I will say that this is what I remember to be the best of my recollection. A woman attorney hired by the Foundation harassed me continually until I gave them the three web sites for thirty dollars. If I had been well informed, I might have charged them thirty thousand dollars.

I never thought that my marriage would fail or that I couldn't be recognized as the expert I worked so diligently to become. It did, and it does, and we move on, finally.

Over the following years, I honed my skills further as a teacher, a writer, a mentor, a friend, and a champion to women that *do not give up* when they know their inner truth. I wrote another best seller this year *Own Your Purpose & Realize Your Potential*, which became an Amazon #1 International Best Seller. I have two more on tap.

We are never given an idea we cannot do. I had the idea, pursued it, and it all worked out, though not exactly as planned.

As for my marriage, had I not made that call to my "financial rep," the result would have been quite different. That woman who raised two amazing children, who was a good wife, who served her community year after year... all of that... that was *not* the end for me!

During those years I sat in the dark and then dealt with the government, I had my eye on a home on a small lake not far from where I was living. When it came on the market, I was unable to purchase it because of my credit score. It was five years later when it came back on the market and my score passed that I was able to buy it. I bought it in 2008 at $100,000, less than it sold for two years before—my first home purchase on my own and I was over 60. I visualized myself over those years until I bought it, living in the home. All the rooms faced the lake and the wrap around deck allowed me to be part of the *eco culture*. It was my dream home.

The next years were all about learning and teaching, and personal development. Already well trained as a coach, I began to look at more and more disciplines, each one making me more aware of my true and infinite potential. I studied transformation, leadership, quantum physics, metaphysics, mind control, spirituality, Abraham-Hicks, the Enneagram... just about all of it. I was full of knowledge and proof that this all worked. Now to figure out a way to do what I loved while make money. The "now" in that sentence came after buying books and programs (many more than I ever read or applied). There was something in the "gathering" of the material and the "throwing of money" at things that didn't want to stop. So, I stopped spending and ran around taking workshops and seminars, filling other people's pockets and thinking about my own legacy and how all I had learned could help women be the role models for our children and grandchildren and be the guardians of wealth and legacy. I stopped and stepped from behind all those things to express my unique voice.

In 2008, I landed on the work of Napoleon Hill (when I

bought LifeSuccess business in a box) and his bestseller *Think and Grow Rich*. For the next five years solid, I studied and facilitated dozens of face to face weekly mastermind studies with 6 to 12 people per study digging deeply into that classic. Some studies I did concurrently and they were not on the same chapter. I was working thirty hours a week in corporate so the mastermind studies I did initially at no charge and then for a modest amount. All great until I retired and had to play for real.

I noticed many of my clients had businesses and were like me. They had a backup plan, whether a husband or a retirement fund. Something. So running a real business was not a priority. On the other hand, I had a weekly paycheck.

People studying Hill's work with me were lit up with the principles of success, and they were getting remarkable results. Most clients were women. We really do thrive when we are learning; it really is the "miracle grow" of life for humans. However, I thought, "Why am I so immersed in this crotchety male content written almost 100 years ago?"

My answer came when I attended a luncheon. There, I saw the results of a report done for our State by the IWPR (Institute of Women's Policy Research) that revealed something so staggering, it caught my attention like a tuning fork—women in our state earn 17.5% less than men, and it would not be until 2054 when the gap collapse on its own based on current statistics.

During that luncheon, I got a hunch or an intuitive *hit* right in my chest. *That* was my answer! The *why*! I was now uniquely qualified to teach those timeless complex concepts women were completely unaware of. Not a clue about the principles of success developed and used by men for more than 200 centuries. The lesson here is to be "watching for" the answer for which you have been asking!

I then spent several years translating the principles and my own teaching platform into a language woman can embrace, creating a unique achievement-driven mastermind program, to first overcome fear by mustering enough courage to do what it takes to earn what they should. That way they could build their businesses to a point of predicting a consistent and growing monthly income, reaping the byproduct of more confidence in business. I explain in Champion why this does not happen for women—they are rarely able to gain traction and momentum in their businesses without certain missing information. It's the missing piece and I love teaching it to women who are willing to do the work.

My women's mastermind is in its twenty-second consecutive business quarter, with measurable, palpable results of women crushing the wage gap every day and building business momentum over the years while remaining happy, healthy and wealthy.

My mission and purpose in 2013 became to crush the wage

gap by 2025, 30 years before expected and to have women ask for what they deserve... and be paid! Moreover, since that time, I have never stopped helping women learn what they never knew and succeed with reliability, predictability and consistency over time.

Early in the first quarter of 2016, I had an idea. I knew if I moved on this idea, I would want all eleven of my VIP mastermind clients to be part of it. The idea was to have a live event for women to empower, inspire and educate those who were ready to grow! We named it *Excelerate Experience*, picked a date in October that year, and began planning an event for women entrepreneurs and small business owners, to teach them the business success principles that are required to achieve success doing 21st century business.

The first hurdle was requiring that each client invest $1,000 each, so we had an operating account with $12,000 to plan the event. I say hurdle because all, except one woman who was an entrepreneur, had experienced an unpredictable and rolling income each month. It took faith to invest nine months in advance in something that could succeed... or could fail.

What they didn't know about me was that I had managed seven annual high school outdoor band competitions with three thousand musicians and families on the field. The planning resulted in some $30,000 dollars for our band program, for uniforms and repairs, competitions, etc.

Agreements signed and venue secure, by October, *Excelerate Experience* had sold out (150 tickets), and I wrote twelve profit checks at Thanksgiving that year. Everyone succeeded.

I repeated the live event in 2017. Slightly profitable, almost all seats sold, entrepreneurs and small business owners were hungry for more learning. Therefore, early that year, we started a monthly lunch and learned to continue our work.

In 2018, the event expanded. It was heart-centered and it attracted speakers from around the US, who answered the question of the event theme, "How do you awaken your infinite potential?" In preparation for the event, I conducted an online telesummit with 26 coaches from around the world in June.

Then I had my own awakening in the middle of the telesummit... "Why not publish a book by transcribing all the interviews?" The message would be powerful because we learn through repetition, and there were 22 examples of "awakenings" and exact first steps "taken" to reach infinite potential.

Everyone agreed and even with everything on our plates, on September 25, 2018 *Own Your Purpose and Realize Your Potential* became #1 International Amazon bestseller for all the authors, a perfect example of mastermind, which is in my wheelhouse. Even in the face of a hurricane, we planned our launch anyway, not allowing any outside condition or circumstance to stop us.

I have learned to get what I want; I only have to remember my grandson at about a year old and his desire to play with his sister and cousins in the "blue" room (playroom) in my home. Only two steps down with a handrail yet it took weeks of trying until he could do it. When he first attempted the steps, he fell flat on his face… more than once! So, we had to be with him and ended up carrying him down the steps each week. When we shut the door to the blue room, he got frustrated and let us know with his regular screaming and crying. We soon turned him around on his tummy, so he could slide down feet first; however, that didn't please him. The next week we put his hand on the rail and held the neck of his shirt, so he could step (float) down, holding on. That went on for about six weeks, and then one day, it happened. After many falls, head first, back first or feet first, he finally did it!

Then guess what he did next that Sunday when his purpose, desire and persistence had finally paid off? Up and down at least twenty-five times that day with him stopping and accepting accolades and applause as he landed, every time. He became a master of those stairs in about an hour.

We must have a very specific and driving desire for something we want very much and to the exclusion of almost all else! That desire drives persistence and ultimately gives us pure faith in ourselves and the results. I learned much of what I already knew about these success principles, but now they were distinguished or revealed to me.

Remember the two-year-old in you. Are you clear about what you really want and why you want it? Will you go to the mat for it? Can you fall deeply in love with it, often to the exclusion of all else? If you can, this is precisely how confidence in our ability and deserve-ability are built. Confidence is a muscle that grows in direct proportion to its use. And the use is in consistent achievement of goals and things we want in spaced intervals over time. If it's a clear goal, it motivates you into action, you know why you want it (what it will provide for you and others), and you start to move toward it before you allow old thoughts "in" to keep you play small, *Go For It*. You will be happy, healthy, and wealthy while you are navigating the obstacles along the way.

If I can do it, so can you.

Chapter 6

RESILIENCE – The REAL Superpower

Tracie L. James

I have always had an amazingly, vivid imagination. So much so that, at times, I would get confused between reality and fantasy. I would create these stories and play them out in great detail… the dialogue, the action, the clothes, the venue. I loved watching television and movies; I would just get lost in the storylines. One of my favorites was the ones about superheroes with amazing superpowers. I wanted to be like them; I wanted to have those amazing abilities. I also liked the idea of having people fear me, or better yet, depend on me to save them. I would be there to save the day just in time, and then everyone would cheer for me.

During my childhood, I pretended to be Wonder Woman, from the Justice League cartoon to Linda Carter's portrayal on TV. I was inspired to be confident, strong, and passionate about protecting people from the evil in the world. I would watch each episode and cheer her on to victory. Looking back, the episodes were so predictable; you know the superhero formula—just when the villain thought they were getting away, they would get defeated by the hero. On Wonder Woman, she was always discounted because she was a woman; they underestimated her strength and her intellect, which ultimately led to their defeat. She always devised a strategy to defeat her enemies. I enjoyed every single episode and remember them until this day.

Deep inside, I wanted to be Wonder Woman in real life; I would spin around trying to turn into her. It never worked, but that didn't stop me from trying. I believed that one day it would work, I just had to do it just right. One time, I got so dizzy from spinning around in my grandmother's living room that I fell and hit my head on the corner of the coffee table. I still have a small scar in the corner of my left eye from that incident. I remember being fussed at for doing it, but it didn't stop me from trying.

I'm sure you're wondering why I was so determined to turn into Wonder Woman. Truthfully, at the time I wasn't really sure. As a kid, I thought it was just fun. Looking back, I have there was so much more to it. I often imagined having my own golden lasso to get people to tell me the truth and then flying away in my invisible jet to my next adventure. I wanted to fly away in my own invisible jet… Don't get me wrong, I had a good childhood, but there was something missing that I couldn't really define at my young age; I just had a strong desire to get away. I wanted to be anywhere except MS. I knew that my Wonder Woman jet could take me anywhere I wanted to go, so I pretended whenever I was alone. Seeing it in hindsight, I realize I was looking for my dad; I didn't meet him until I was 29. It took me years to get up the nerve to ask about him and why he wasn't around. I assumed for so long that he wasn't there because he didn't want me, but I eventually found out he didn't know I had been born. I spent most of my life in search of his love and acceptance. I needed to be Wonder Woman to get the truth and go find him. Once I found him, I initially didn't know how to process the truth I found…

My love of superheroes didn't stop in childhood. It stayed with me as I got older, but in a slightly different way. I started to look for examples in real life for superpowers I could acquire. As a teen, I wanted to be Debbie Allen—she is an amazing dancer, choreographer, actress, singer, director, producer, etc… The list goes on and on. My weekends were spent watching her on the TV show *Fame*. I danced along with her on the show and wanted to dress in leotards and dance skirts. She was one of the reasons I wanted to join the dance/drill team in junior high school. I was now focused on becoming her; she became my superhero of choice. I could follow her path and get out of MS.

I did my research on her life and decided I was going to do what she did—attend Howard University and major in theatre and dance, then go on to New York to dance on Broadway. I buckled down and worked really hard in school to get the grades to get into one the top Black Ivy League schools in the country. I was elated when I received my acceptance letter to Howard just as my senior year in high school began. I was so ready to get out of the state and follow my dreams of becoming my superhero.

When I was 17 and entering my senior year in high school, I felt on top of the world. I was convinced that it was going to be a perfect year. I had been elected Miss Jim Hill High School and Student Government Vice President. In addition, I was selected as Captain of the Tigerette Dance Team. To top it off, I began the school year as number one in my class. As far as I was concerned, things could not get any better.

A few months into my senior year, my plans began to fall apart...

First, I was accepted, but I didn't receive a full scholarship to Howard. As a result, I had to figure out how to pay for the balance of my tuition, fees, room & board, etc. Remember, I was raised by a single mother...

Second, I found out I was pregnant in November 1989. The smart girl was pregnant. The leader was pregnant. The perfect one was not so perfect any more. What was I going to do? I was afraid and confused and I had to figure out what was next in my life and how I could still become my superhero.

I was faced with another major challenge at 17. How do you make a decision concerning an unplanned pregnancy? I am a talker, but I did not know to whom I should talk about this situation. I was all over the place. I was angry with myself. I cried. I screamed. I wanted to hide my pregnancy until I had decided what to do, which is what I did for almost 4 months.

Eventually, I had to face it and talk with my family. That was no easy task, but I did it with tears streaming. My family rose to the occasion and fully supported me on this difficult journey. Of course, they were disappointed, but they made sure I knew they loved me and believed in me. My mother wanted me to know she understood how I felt. She had me when she was only 19 years old. My grandparents stressed the importance that I not give up on my plans for college; they believed in education and wanted me to know they would help me get my degree. My mind was set that I was graduating with my class and going on to college. My life at home was great. I was loved and supported.

Once it became public knowledge that I was pregnant, there was a lot of negativity swirling around me. At times, it was hard to handle. I was determined to hold my head high no matter what anyone said to my face or behind my back. To this day, I'm amazed at what people had the nerve to say to me. Not just the kids in my class, but adults too. "Your life is over." "You are so stupid." "You should just drop out of school and get your GED." This made me feel so worthless and it made me so hurt and angry.

I was dying inside, but I couldn't let anyone see it. I put on my cape, placed the "S" on my chest and pretended nothing they said or did bothered me. I will admit that there were days I didn't even want to get out of bed. I wanted to just lie there and cry, but I pressed through. I dried my tears and got dressed for school. I remained focused on my goal to graduate with my class, give my valedictory speech and go on to college.

On June 6, 1990, I stood on that stage and delivered my speech. I was 9 months pregnant and my son was expected to arrive any day. I proudly shared a message of hope for the future with my classmates; it was a beautiful, joyful day that I will never forget. It is still one of the highlights of my life. The next one happened just two weeks later when I became a mother for the first time at 18. I never knew you could love someone so much until I had my first son. He was perfect and I was happy to be his mom.

The next phase of my life truly tested my superpowers— teen mom and college student.

Before my first year of college started, I let go of my dream of becoming my superhero Debbie Allen. I was told so often to get a real degree so I could get a real job with benefits and stability that I finally gave in. I changed my major to Business Administration then to Marketing and focused on taking on the business world. I had to find my superpower in business, but I had no idea where to even start.

Personally, all I wanted was the super power to be bullet-proof... or at least *wordproof*. I allowed the words and opinions of others to affect me. I wore the tough mask like it didn't bother me, but when I was alone, I cried. It was tough to attend college in your hometown with everyone thinking they knew who you were and what was happening in your life. My name was mentioned in neighborhood gossip because I had my son at 18. I won't even share the names I was called behind my back and often even to my face by people I once considered friends. The betrayals cut me deep in the midst of letting go of my dream of dancing on Broadway.

The coursework was hard enough to tackle while learning how to be a mom. Learning how to be myself in the midst of feeling criticized for how I was living my life was even harder. I struggled with my self-esteem and self-worth. Deep down, I had never forgiven myself for not making better decisions concerning sex. I loved my son, but I struggled with guilt for having him so young. I was in no way prepared for what moth-erhood entailed. I also didn't like hearing that people *knew* I was going to get pregnant young because my mother had me at 19. What a horrible prophecy to speak over a child! Looking back, I wonder if I just lived up to what was expected of me.

At one point, I decided to just live my life freely and not worry about what people thought of me. I said it, but it's not how I really felt on the inside. I would do things to get people to like me and later feel awful because I didn't live by any standards. I allowed people to treat me any way they chose to, often without any consequence. Publicly, I would stand tall and strong so most felt I was the type of person you couldn't take advantage of... but privately there were people I loved that lied to me, cheated on me, and manipulated me to get what they wanted without regard to my feelings. The crazy thing is that I allowed it because I just wanted them to love me. The way they treated me didn't show me that they loved me; it showed me they didn't really care about me. Looking back, I realize that, but at the time I couldn't see it. There are people who really loved me that I pushed away because I didn't know how to receive their love. How could they love me when I didn't love me?

Somehow, I not only survived college, but I thrived... at least academically. I graduated with honors and began my career in retail management. My new dream was to be a successful retail buyer for a major retailer in the US. I was on my way and hoping to fast track my career.

Entering the work world, I thought I had found my superpower—I was, and still am, a chameleon. I have the ability to fit into any environment I'm placed in. This superpower helped me build my career in corporate America for many years. I was the youngest, only black, only female in many situations. I had no problem adjusting in these arenas... not just adjusting, but thriving. I was the person that could get people on board with the new plan, new product or new process with ease. I did my research. I paid attention to people and what they liked and disliked. I created my presentation accordingly and got the deal done. I got the team on board. My superpower made me a powerhouse in sales.

As much success as this superpower brought me in my career, being a chameleon was kryptonite in my personal life. It manifested itself in being a people pleaser. I kept changing myself so much that I eventually lost sight of who I really was. It destroyed romantic relationships and crippled friendships; it wasn't their fault that I didn't present who I really was to them in these relationships. I just wanted them to like me or rather love me so much that I changed myself into who I "thought" they wanted me to be. Many times, I became who they said they wanted me to be. You can change yourself, but eventually the real you will come out and completely destroy the image they had of you. You can't stay in their box forever. It's just too uncomfortable.

The downside of being a chameleon was never more evident than it was in my marriage. I got married quickly after a very short courtship. I quickly realized that my decision was not well-thought-out, so I considered getting a divorce after only a couple of months of marriage. Our marriage was in no way like our courtship. We went from talking nonstop to barely able to communicate. Before I could file for divorce, I found out I was pregnant. This changed everything. I made a decision to stay and try to work things out for our child's sake.

The next two years of my life were so tough. The constant arguments pressed me so hard that I stopped talking honestly. I just said what I felt he wanted me to say to just keep the peace. I kept changing myself in hopes that eventually I would become who he wanted me to be so the verbal assaults would stop. Unfortunately, no matter how much I changed it never seemed to be enough. Hiding who I truly was inside became harder and harder. The day finally came when I could no longer bite my tongue for the sake of keeping the peace. I finally started to do me, and as a result, we remained in conflict. One day it all came to a head and we decided it was best for us to part ways. It was a hard decision because I didn't like to fail at anything. That caused me to feel like a failure all over again.

After going through my divorce and being faced with entering my 40s, I took time to get to know Tracie. I needed to know who she really was if I was going to live the life I was created to live. I couldn't get to my purpose until I took an hon-

104

est look at who I was at my core. I had heard people talk about it, but I hadn't really considered it until I found myself ending an affair with a married man... I had finally done what I said I would never do. I was determined to never make the same mistake again, and I took drastic measures to ensure I wouldn't.

In 2014, I took a hiatus from dating. I realized that I was making the same mistakes in relationships and I kept dating the exact same guy. I was sick of doing so... That guy was not necessarily a bad guy; he just wasn't good for me. I had to break the cycle so I took a break from dating and began to get to know myself for the first time. I had jumped from one bad relationship to the next throughout my dating life, never taking more than a few months in between to be by myself.

In the midst of this self-reflection, I learned that my *real* superpower is my resilience. I don't give up. I may get knocked down, but eventually I get back up. One of the things that my coach told me he admires about me is my ability to keep stepping up to bat no matter how many times I strike out. Disappointment and rejection may slow me down, but in the end, I get up, dust myself off and keep moving forward. The foundation of my resilience is my faith in God. His Spirit inside of me presses me forward towards my purpose.

My Strategies to Build Resilience

In life, there will be times where we will be rejected—jobs, relationships, etc. We all have to deal with not getting what we want in life at times; nevertheless, how you deal with it is the true test of being successful. People who are resilient get through these times better. It's so important to develop resilience because it is your ability to bounce back from disappointment and painful situations that occur in life. How well do you bounce back from being rejected?

One of the most important keys we must have is the power of resilience. You must develop a love for yourself enough to fight for yourself no matter what happens. You must make a decision to have the courage to push through whatever you're going through. To never give up on you, even when it doesn't look like it's going to work out. Discover the superhero inside of you. *You* are your own superhero.

Understand Resilience

Resilience is defined as the capacity to withstand life's stresses, challenges, and catastrophes. It is the ability to bounce back, to rise, and to cope when others fall apart under the same set of challenges. There is a quote by Maya Angelou that I love and I actually have it on my wall. "Surviving is important, but thriving is elegant." Thriving is my goal in life. I hit a point in my life where I decided to stop surviving and embrace thriving. I haven't looked back since.

You can never be happy in life if you do not know how to

successfully rebound from life's storms. It's not if storms will come, but when. You must be prepared for the storms and be ready to stand against them.

These factors can help you build resilience:

- Close relationships with family and friends.

- Embrace your value, your worth.

- Effectively manage strong feelings and impulses.

- Develop conflict resolution skills.

- Control of your emotions.

- Take personal responsibility for your choices and actions.

- Avoid having a victim mentality.

- Develop positive ways to cope with stress.

- Being optimistic and looking for the good in even the worst situation.

Find Your Resilience

Be intentional when dealing with rejection. Carolyn Gregoire, in her article *How to Bounce Back from Failure—Over and Over Again*, outlines seven traits that resilient people possess:

- They are realistic but are also optimistic.

- They don't take rejection personally.

- They create strong support systems.

- They notice the "small," positive things of life, like flowers or running streams of water.

- They practice gratitude daily.

- They seek out opportunities to improve and grow as people.

- They work through their emotions and feelings instead of avoiding them.

Look at yourself honestly and see how many of these traits do you possess. Which of these traits can you develop with focused effort? We must live with a growth mindset… we can change.

Take some time to think about rejections you dealt with in your life. Assess them honestly by answering these questions:

- What was the worst part about being rejected?

- What were the benefits of being rejected?

- Which rejection(s) permanently ruined your life and/or ability to be successful?

Once you answer these questions, you will then be able

With Inspiring Stories

to see how resilient you really are and continue to grow and develop your resilience muscle. The more adversity you face and the less you give up, the stronger your resilience muscle will become. It's just like working out—the more you do it, the stronger you will get. Keep stepping up to bat and try your best to knock it out of the park!

Chapter 7

LIVE THE LIFE YOU WANT. "Reveal the masterpiece within you. The time to take action is now!"

Divya Parekh

Your Story

Whether you live your life with awareness or lack of awareness, you live it. Whether you want to make an impact or not, you are doing it because your friends, family, community, and environment are influenced by the life you live. When you live the life you want, you find joy and fulfillment. Moreover, you create a lasting impact on others. I will share my story and fundamental principles that will help you live the life you want.

My Story

My journey to embracing love and relationships as the centerpiece of my teachings began with my liberal upbringing in India. My parents encouraged my sister and me to be forward thinking; they taught us that there were no limiting gender boundaries and helped us realize our full potential. I was fortunate to have parents who pushed me and my sister. They took every opportunity to show us practical lessons of life as well as encouraging our academic work. Their methods were different, however. For example, we had a farm across the way from our house where I grew up. There was a neem tree on the property that people wanted to cut down and use for their benefit. You see, the neem tree is a natural antiseptic and has various medicinal uses. When people found an unattended tree, it would be immediately cut down. My father would educate us by hugging that tree and teach us its uses; he would tell us why people shouldn't cut it down, especially since it did belong to the owner of the land whether he was there or not.

My mother, on the other hand, saw us in much bigger roles for our lives than we dared dream for ourselves at the time. Her larger-than-life vision gave us a push to what we set out to do in life. I was fortunate to have parents who encouraged us. My dad was usually more laidback than my mom; however, they complemented each other well because if I did not feel like I did not live up to the highest expectations of my mom, I could get down on myself. That was when my Dad's words came in handy because he would say to me, "Your mom has her vision and does a lot for you. She also expects a lot from you, and that makes you strive for more. However, if you fail or fall short, her disappointment is on her, not you!" My dad was one of my biggest and best teachers.

India is a land of diverse cultures, different languages, religious beliefs, yoga and meditation, compassion, and much more. I grew up with reflection and exposure to cultural diversity at home, school, and in society, so meditating became a way of life rather than a chore. It helped me to dream big, define my vision, lay the groundwork for clarity and purpose, and then start my journey with the discipline to stay the course. When I moved to the United States to continue my education here, it was a smooth transition because students and professors were from different cultures and welcomed me into their world. Because the seed of connectivity was planted in me early in life, I felt like I was one of them, and soon we were arguing the merits of the Yankees versus the Mets.

Science has had a draw for me. I very much enjoy figuring out how and why things work a certain way. In my biochemistry studies, I learned about the interconnection between body, mind, and intellect. I began my career as a university associate professor of chemistry and biochemistry, splitting my time between leading research efforts and teaching graduate students. I left academia and entered the world of research labs and biopharmaceutical organizations. There, I had opportunities to show my leadership in program management, team leading, process engineering, personnel, and partnership development.

The corporate world was tough at times; I had to balance

family and career, and this is never an easy process. There were days I wanted to throw the towel in and quit. It was then that the fire of being something larger than myself kicked into my weariness. That desire would get me through the rough patches. The key thing that I learned was the "*Why* you are doing something" has to be the "*Why* of your life." This is true, not just for your career or your business, but of everything in life. When you grasp this organic approach to all facets of life, it makes you strive to do your best in all areas.

I began to develop a passion for coaching. My unbridled desire to make a positive impact on people led me to believe my true calling in life is to help leaders, entrepreneurs, and achievers see their genius, reveal their masterpiece, and craft their message of significance. It led to a merger of my bio-pharmaceutical career with coaching to develop effective evidence-based leadership and partnership programs. I had the opportunity to work with several pharmaceutical and financial organizations and help them achieve the results they wanted. The relationships and connections I build with people is the icing on the cake, making my life more productive and fuller.

Relationships

The substance of everything I teach is that you need to focus on your vision of what you want and that you mindfully develop relationships of significance with yourself and others to achieve it. You might underestimate the power you have to design your life. You might feel stuck in your personal or professional life. That said, I have discovered through my own experience, and by helping others learn to develop the types of relationships I have, that you can achieve professional and personal fulfillment at the same time. These connections allow us to bring more joy, more love, and more freedom to our lives.

A word here on mindfulness. As a definition, mindfulness is a conscious choice of living in the present, guided by value-based decisions and non-judgments. Mindfulness is also living with grace. As we focus on our goals, grace weaves its way into day-to-day activities and relationships.

Mindfulness brings self-awareness without judgment. Knowing yourself is the foundation of authenticity. Non-judgment allows you to be accepting of your strengths and limitations. You are open to finding out about your blind spots and emotional hindrances. You can turn them into assets, driven by the values and support of friends and mentors. Mindfulness makes you want to grow and allows you to learn from your life experiences—failures and successes alike — while retaining humility.

It is necessary to exercise mindfulness as you explore the relationships you have with yourself and others. Some relationships may be more natural; others might take more effort. Regardless, the more you concentrate and work on a relationship, the easier it will be to integrate into your life. We will explore now the nine essential relationships (self, time, money, market, team, partners, death, results, and legacy) that, when illuminated in our consciousness and when embraced with grace and mindfulness, give us access to the humility and the potential for resilient altruism that is a prerequisite for sharing oneself with others. These serve as the foundational bedrock for developing relationships and connections with others.

Relationship with Self

You might be saying, "I understand that you need to have relationships with various people to have success in your life's work, but what do you mean a relationship with yourself?"

We do need relationships to do what we want in life. First, we need to have a clear understanding of ourselves before we can do anything. You must be clear on the values and message you share with yourself and others. With clarity, you will be empowered and prepare yourself for the desired outcome. Developing this relationship with yourself empowers you to speak out and communicate authentically. It is the crucial stepping-stone to developing superb leadership skills.

Relationship with self is the underpinning of your life's joy, freedom, and success. When you let core values and mindfulness be your guiding compass, you:

• Will be able to stand up for yourself without being a doormat.

- Will be able to forgive others for your own sake and take the lessons learned from experiences to grow yourself and others.

- Will increase your self-trust, self-confidence, and achieve peak performance.

- Will, overall, build a rock-solid foundation that will weather both good and challenging times with equanimity.

Relationship with Time

One of my coaching clients, Lina, had a misguided relationship with time. She mistook busy for being productive. She couldn't understand how she could work 12 hours a day and not seem to get anywhere. She had started her own software company and got frustrated at the inequity between her daily activity and profits.

As we worked together, Lina realized that time is the most valuable currency of life. The key to understanding a relationship with time is knowing where you are in your life right now, and where your personal and professional life is going to be in the long term. Once Lina's vision for her life became clear, she was able to use her time wisely by minimizing distractions and taking the *right* actions. Her company began to thrive, and she had had more free time to enjoy the fruits of her labor.

Relationship with Money

People can have a complicated relationship with money. It is crucial to think about what your relationship with money is, especially when you want to increase your profits substantially. It's great to earn it, but it is better to understand early on how to discipline yourself in its use. What you do with your money is the most critical component of your relationship with it.

Nothing illustrates more of a person's nature than what they do with money, particularly when they have either an extreme abundance or scarcity of it. When you align vision and values with personal and professional life, you can achieve balance. This connection carries over to money. Your money mindset allows you to know what having money means and that money is not evil. It gives you the freedom to be mindfully aware of the present moment while knowing that your decisions and actions determine the results.

Your money mindset is going to determine the league you play in. If you think small, you are going to work with clients who want to play in a minor league or take opportunities that keep you in your comfort zone. If you believe that there is no limit to your business growth, your efforts will focus on clients who want you to help them grow to the next level. You will also seek out opportunities that will catapult you to unimagined levels. Once you bring all your values into your work, your business will grow exponentially.

Relationship with Market

The relationship with money motivated me to understand my market. Knowing your market is essential whether you have your own business or are an executive in a large corporation. We all have a market depending on our business niche. Relationship with the market is knowing and understanding your ideal client, establishing your brand, making a positive impact, and serving your clients to help them succeed in their personal, professional, and financial goals. By aligning yourself with your market, you can provide the best solutions for your clients in your area of expertise.

I have had more than one client who felt like they were spinning their wheels trying to grow their business. Many times, the solution was to help them realize their company did not know or understand their customers well. I helped them build a loyal customer base by shifting their shotgun approach of trying to be everything to everybody to one of connecting and forming relationships with those who could benefit the most from their products or services.

Relationship with Team

When you work with people to achieve a common goal, a healthy relationship with your team is essential. Within a team, the leader is the catalyst that drives his or her team to thrive, so each member provides extreme value both individually and

118

collectively. If you are the leader of a team, you are responsible for strengthening the relationship among the team members.

When I work with organizational or business teams, I help them become high performing teams with humanistic values. The focus is on purpose, encouragement, real-time feedback, and reinforcing structures. Happy team members play a significant role in each other's personal, professional, and financial success because they help accomplish the team's and the company's goals. When you work as a collaborative team, everybody is involved in planning, designing, developing, and implementing those goals. When you achieve the goals, the entire team cheers and celebrates. After all, they helped make it happen!

When you have a connected team, the contributions and support enable you to orchestrate productivity, innovation, creativity, and the best quality products and services. This profitability enhances everyone's life.

Relationship with Partners

Business is a system in which all parts and processes contribute to the success or failure of the whole. We all work with other professionals outside of our organization or business; these specialists or contractors help us with various aspects of our company. You might want partners who share in every aspect of your company, from initial establishment to sustainable success, or the purpose may be to work together for one particular project. The partner could be someone who specializes in a different industry than yours, but his or her company complements yours perfectly because they bring a different perspective to business operations. By joining forces, you grow together.

Whatever your intention is with a partner, it is important to realize that it is about collaborating, not competing. You are pooling resources of the mind and heart. With your partner, you want to create more opportunities, create more emotional and financial wealth, and go beyond what you can do alone. It also means that you sometimes need to have difficult conversations if you have people who are not keeping up their end of the bargain.

For example, I formed a partnership with a book publisher, and we put together a written contract. The contract defined clear expectations including the roles and responsibilities of both parties; however, the publisher failed to deliver their end of the agreement. After several unsuccessful attempts to salvage the relationship, I decided to cut them loose. Sometimes, working on a relationship with a partner involves limiting your losses before things become irreparable.

Relationship with Death

As they say, nothing is certain except death and taxes. Our 21st-century society tries to insulate us from death. However, proximity to death or failure forces us to explore our fears and feelings about the subject. Doing so gives us the opportunity to live our lives in a new and fulfilling manner.

This relationship is about accepting fear, working through it, and using the grit that you have deep inside of you to overcome it. It is about living life rather than passing through it. Shakespeare said, "A coward dies a thousand times before his death, but the valiant taste of death but once." By establishing your relationship with death, you learn to live with that fear in your life. It will help you overcome challenges, go after new opportunities, and set your affairs to take care of your loved ones and your business in the event of your death.

Relationship with Results

Your connection with results matters! Results are the milestones that tell us if we're going in the right direction. Success requires destination and destination need direction. Life is a journey comprised of many goals. It is about living a mindful life driven by value-based decisions, learning, unlearning, and relearning while having fun. The relationship with results is how you measure success, clearly defining outcomes, determining progress, and learning from failures as you work toward your goals.

This relationship can take on many forms. I have worked with people who did not know how to handle their success.

121

They didn't know what to do with it, how to continue it, or how to leverage it into significant positive results. Think of that as you get closer to achieving your goals. Are you going to know what to do once you get there?

I had issues with my results when starting in my coaching career. I was working with great clients and having a degree of success regarding activity and income, but I wasn't happy with it. I evaluated my business growth and mindfully applied the lessons learned from successes and failures. This helped me scale up my business; I went from coaching individual clients to coaching teams and departments in bigger companies. Being comfortable in the relationship with my results allowed me to speak to several hundred people at once and write books to help many others.

Relationship with Legacy

Finally, there is the relationship with legacy. Usually, when we think of a legacy, it is what we leave behind after we leave this world. We all like to believe others will remember us because of what we will leave behind. This is true to an extent, but you can start your legacy *now*! Empowerment has a ripple effect—your fiery message can ignite a passion in someone else. Every time you act as a leader with your message, you enable others to choose challenges with courage.

There is so much you can do today that will leave an

impression on someone's future. It might be working with kids, seniors, or animals. It can be working with a local nonprofit or being on the board of a national organization. You never know when giving of yourself is going to impact a person's future. You might not even know them personally, but your efforts could change someone's life forever.

My Legacy

Part of what I teach others and advocate in my own life is creating a sustained solution. I donate a portion of my books' profits to KIVA, which is an international nonprofit connecting people through lending to alleviate poverty. By giving as little as $25 to Kiva, anyone can help a borrower start or grow a business, go to school, access clean energy, or realize their potential. For some, it's a matter of survival; for others, it's the fuel for a life-long ambition.

I take a great interest in the lives of our youth. I do not look at it as a cliché but as truth—children are our future. In some places, our youth have limited access to educational opportunities that could shape their lives and community for the better. I prefer to partner with organizations that take a systematic approach to address root issues rather than slap a Band-Aid on a problem. So, I partner with TMT Youth Community Foundation, a nonprofit organization that focuses on accessing, developing, and growing the talents of young people. I also collaborate with The Little Maker's Academy that focuses on collaborative learning and critical thinking with young students through hands-on STEAM activities.

I also work with Inspire NC, a student-led non-profit organization whose aim is to promote interest, knowledge, and involvement in the fields of STEAM and develop leadership in the next generation. Through Inspire NC, I mentor a Robotics Team. These young people build and operate robots. They have fun doing it… I don't know how many of them will become great scientists or engineers in the future, but I know what I do is having an impact on their lives.

My work with relationships is one of my legacies, and I take seriously the contribution I make to others' lives. I believe that when you make a difference in your life, a loved one's life, or someone else's, one blend into another. When you are confident in your passion, you work at it. I have a passion for making a difference. I want to reach out and genuinely help others. I find opportunities to do that every day whether it is something small or a larger endeavor. Let today become the springboard for empowering love in your and others' lives every day.

Live the Life You Want

Grateful I am,
For who I am.
Today, I am,
Ready to take on tomorrow.
When I look back on today,
I have no sorrow.
Right or wrong, choices I will make,
Every day, for my sake
Action over inaction
Purpose, pain, and passion
Learning to unlearn and relearn
Prepared for what awaits me,
Around every corner, I turn.
Support each other,
and grow together.
Build relations
And bridge nations.
Live your legacy.
There's no fallacy.
Achieving success, happier than ever.
Reducing our stress in this joyful endeavor.
The future is now our present.
Nimbly unwrap your return on investment.

Chapter 8

One woman, one voice, one journey, searching for a way...

Rose Jones

S ilence is the world of the unknown, a world that conquer most. It surrounded me with so many people, yet I stood alone. Left to drown in my deepest thoughts, fears and tormented trauma. My mental state went into survival mode, fighting every day for my freedom. Lost, confused, and not knowing what to do or what to say. Consumed with worry about what people may say, how they would feel about me or treat me, if they will believe me, and most importantly, still love me. I found myself lost with nowhere to go and stuck in a reality that was very toxic, yet that was all I knew. So deep into silence... will I ever get out?

You're probably wondering how someone could get stuck so deep into their silence that it literally consumed their whole being, how can someone allow themselves to get stuck in this state for so long. It's very easy to put yourself into a place where you're not aware of what's going on or how to help yourself.

It begins with me as a young child. I started my childhood like a traditional family—my mother and father were married, we owned our own house and my mother was the all-American housewife, always cooking, cleaning and taking care of the kids; on the other hand, my father used to work his 9-5 and paid the bills. They had four beautiful children—two boys and two girls who went to school and got good grades.

Sadly, that didn't last long; I can remember the shift in family atmosphere when I was six years old. My father started to become more aggressive and jealous toward my mother, yelling, throwing things at her and even hitting her. I also recall coming home from church on Sunday and my father instantly getting upset with my mother because we arrived home late because the church van had a few extra stops. Then, my father started to accuse my mother of sleeping with the pastor. She tried to explain to him what happened, but he didn't want to hear it. He took my mother to the bedroom and all you could hear was bagging and yelling; it continued for about an hour. Afterwards, he exited the room and told my mother to stay there, think about what she did and fix herself up. He came in the living, sat on the sofa, and watched the football game like nothing ever happened. About 15 minutes later, my mother came out the room and went straight to the kitchen to start cooking dinner, and then we continued our day like normal. That became our daily routine.

After a while, he turned on us and we became his target as well. He didn't hit us, but he yelled at us and accused us of telling our family and neighbors our family business. He would say, "What goes on in this house, stays here. If I find out you said anything, there will be consequences". We believed him, and since we didn't want to find out what would happen if we opened our mouths, we stayed quiet. Still to this day, this is my first-time talking about my family problems with anyone other than my siblings or people that might have witnessed the abuse. My father died in 2015 and, in some way, he still controls my thoughts and my words from the grave. He was cremated, and I decided to give all his children, sister, brother, and grandchildren a necklace with his ashes in them. I kept the rest of the ashes. If you're wondering why did I do that, the answer will come soon.

After a while, despite my mother's efforts, our traditional family was no longer the middle-class loving family. My father picked up a strong drug addiction, bills weren't getting paid, we lost the house and the car, me and my siblings started to misbehave, and divorce came soon after. We quickly became a lower-class family, and fell into the society's stereotype of a tra-ditional African-American family—a single mother working 60-80 hours a week to support her family, children considered below average in school because they were stuck in a school system that doesn't care, and living in someone else's home (paying rent).

That transition weighted a lot on me. I lost everything and everyone I had ever known, and I had to get used to a whole new life. It left me confused and feeling unloved and lost; I didn't understand what was going on. All I knew was that mommy and daddy no longer loved each other. My mother and father never sat down with us to explain what had happened, which made my mind go into circles. I didn't know what to do; however, what I definitely knew was that I wasn't going to say anything to anyone because I was scared of what could happen. I continued living my life as normal as I could, trying to bring the joys of my old life back, but that never happen. As I got older, life got harder. I had already lost my father and I was slowly losing my mother. She was never home because of work, and when she was home, she wasn't really present; in addition, she started dating again. When she divorced my father, it felt as if she divorced me too.

I became insecure, had low self-esteem, lacked of confidence, and I didn't know my self-worth. I was so lost, overwhelmed and confused that I started to search for ways to fill the gaps in my life. However, I didn't know what I was missing to make me a whole. I was still a child looking up to my family for guidance and I crossed path with a family member that decided to use my lack of knowledge, understanding as an option to prey on me. He said that I needed someone to love me and he was willing to show me what real love was. He took that opportunity to do things to me that stole my childhood away. While it was happening, I knew it was wrong, I knew that was something I shouldn't be experiencing at that age; nevertheless, I didn't have the strength or courage to say no or stop him. When he was finished, he said, "This is our little secret, don't tell no one. We are family, so family business stays with family." That created a new level of confusion in my head. I wanted love, but not that type of love. When I thought about telling someone what had happened, his words kept repeating in my head, "This is our little secret, don't tell no one." I knew from past experiences that if you tell family business, there can be dire consequences. So, I decided to keep the little secret.

He thought that, since I kept the secret, I was okay with that, so he continued abusing me. He got so comfortable with abusing me that he would even touch me in front of my mother. I remember the first time he did it. I was in my room and my mother was in the kitchen cooking dinner. He came into my room and tried to touch me, and I said I had to pee, so I ran into the kitchen with mother and started a conversation. I guess he heard me, because he came in soon after. While my mother's back was turned as she cooked on the stove, he stood behind my chair and put his hands down my shirt. Every time my mother turned her back, I would give my mother a weird look, but she didn't catch on. Either she thought I was being silly, or she just didn't care at that moment; I knew that that would never end. As I got older, I learned how to avoid him, and after a while, he gave up or found another victim.

That became like a trend in my life, I felt like the word *easy target* was stamped on my forehead. I was so insecure and scared, that people could probably smell it. Every time a guy approached to talk to me alone, said that they had a secret to tell, or wanted to tell me to smile because I was too beautiful to frown, my heart would race, and my hands would shake. My mind would tell me to run the other way, but for some reason, my feet followed them. These men were older guys, my sibling's friends. However, these guys didn't want to have sex, they just wanted to touch me. They would sneak into my room, act like they just wanted to talk to me and were interested in what I was doing, and then they would just start touching me. I would walk to the store and hear my name being called on the side of the house, which always ended up with me being touched. That continued for a while until I was old enough to distance myself and hide.

I'm going to press pause on my story right now because I want my reader to truly experience what I'm going through as I write about some of my life experiences. I'm literally putting myself out there for everyone one to see and judge. I have been through so much pain and grief that I'm not sure if I can take any more rejection. So, to be truly honest, I want to stop right here because the next part of my story causes me so much pain that I'm so scared to experience this level of hate and confusion again. I worked so hard to become the person that I am today and I don't want my hard work to be discredited or overshined by a dark period of my life. Let's pause again… Just thinking about it is causing me an anxiety attack… I can't stop crying. My heart won't stop racing, my hands are shaking… I have to call my boyfriend and my sister for words of encouragement and strength to get me through this moment.

Okay. After talking to both of them, they set my mind at rest. They said "this is my story to tell and it's not fair to tell half of the story." Either tell it all or walk away, and I'm not even going to lie to you, at first I decided to walk away. I stopped writing my chapter, but as time got closer and closer to submitting the chapter, I started to build up the courage and strength to finish because it doesn't matter what people said about me. I will never allow anyone or anything to drag me back to the place of silence ever again. So, I speak on!

This part of my story starts a little different. There was one guy in my life that I looked up to like a brother—my older sister's boyfriend, Mr. A. I felt like he cherished me and didn't really wanted anything from me other than for me to be happy. Every time I would look sad, he would try to cheer me up saying powerful words like "Don't give up, tomorrow will be better," "Stop looking down all the time, that's why you keep bumping your head," or "Who hurt your feelings? I'll beat them up for you." You know, things a big brother would say to his little sister. I remember telling him about my family hitting hard times and my mother couldn't afford to buy me anything, and he quickly volunteered to buy those things for me. I was so excited and happy that somebody wanted to do something for me. Sometimes I thought he was doing it to get on my sister's good side and to look good in front of the family. He would also make sure to say bye to me; he made me feel comfortable being around the opposite sex for the first time in my life. As time went on, we got closer and closer. I could talk to him about anything, so I thought someone in my life finally loved me; he never said it, but I just felt loved in his presence.

However, that quickly changed when I started to have boy-friends. I could feel his energy changing towards me; he always seemed to be mad at me and I couldn't understand why. I was very used to rejection, so I knew when someone didn't want to be bothered. Once again, I kept my distance for a while. Summer break came around and I spent most of the summer at my sister's house. There, we started to reconnect again. He explained to me why he was mad—he didn't like that I was dating those boys that were using me because I was too spe-cial to be treated that way. What he didn't know was that I wasn't doing anything with those boys; I would never allow myself to be alone with anybody. He had heard some rumors

133

that were being spread about me and, being honest, I couldn't have cared less. I was so used to being people's punching bag that it became a part of my daily life; it didn't even bother me anymore. In the meantime, I was shocked that he cared about how other people treat me. People usually don't care about me. At that moment, I thought he wanted to protect me from being hurt. My luck seemed to be changing, I have someone that was looking out for me. Now I'm no longer alone.

About halfway through the summer, I started dating a boy and I had the biggest crush on him. I didn't think he would ever be interested in me, so when he approached me, I was shocked and even speechless that he wanted to get to know me. We would sit on my sister's porch for hours talking. Then, one day, he kissed me and all hell broke loose. Mr. A. stormed out of the house in a rage, telling my boyfriend to go home and never come back. He also told me to go upstairs, and then took me into the room, sitting me down. He started to give a long lecture about respect and whatever else; I wasn't listening because I was angry, so I let him talk while waiting for the moment to leave. I didn't understand why I was in that room and why he felt he had the right to control what I did; I was confused and mad. I finally muscled up the guts to ask him if he was done and if I could leave. He looked at me with anger in his eyes and then calmly said these words to me "You don't get it, do you? I love you." My respond was, "I get you love me as sister and you want the best for me." His respond was "You weren't listening to me, I love you and I want to show how much I love you." At that moment my body was paralyzed, I didn't know what to do. I couldn't speak or move, so I just sat there in shock as I allowed him to have his way with me. Every part of me knew that was wrong, but no part of me could stop it. After he was done, I wanted to go home, so I called my mom. I was babysitting my sister's kids, I couldn't leave. When my sister got home, I debated with myself whether I should tell her or not. Then, he walked past by me with a look on his face that said it all. I was ready to go back home and do what I do best—hide and hope it all go away. But… I knew this wasn't going to go away. I was able to distance myself for a while because school started again and I became super impossible to track down.

Then, they moved a few blocks away from me, so he started to spend a lot of time at my house. I kept my distance, but he figured out a way to find me. He started being at my bus stop, walking me home from school and asking me about my day, and writing me love letters. Those wired feelings started to overcome me; I knew it was wrong to feel that way, but I didn't know what to do about it. I couldn't talk to anyone about what had happened to me or about what was currently happening to me. I was alone. As time went on, he continued being around me and I became less restricted, starting to accept the fact that he would probably not give up anytime soon. When he saw my guards started to weaken, he took his option to prey on me again and again. I instantly threw my guards back up and started dating, which made him mad, scaring away anyone I would try to get close to me. It got so bad I stopped doing it... I stopped being interested in the thought of being happy.

Not even six months later, he kept asking me this question, "Did your *Aunt Flo* come this month?" and I didn't know what he was talking about, so I looked at him with a confused look on my face. Then he explained to me what he meant, "Did you have your period this month?" After his question, I realized I didn't and there could be a chance that I was pregnant. I went to the doctor with my best friend and the test came back positive. I held my tears back in the doctor's office, but when I got home, I cried for days. I was not ready to be a mother, I was only a sophomore in high school... how was I going to explain that to my family? My mind went into protective mode; I had to find a way to protect myself from the wrath that was going to hit my way when everyone found out.

I immediately started to date a guy and I brought him around the family trying to set up my escape plan and hoping that I could convince everyone that it could be his baby. As the months went by, belly started to show, so I knew I had to tell my family. I told my cousin just to get a little relief, but by the time I went home from school, my whole family knew. I felt betrayed. Not knowing what to say or do, I told them I was pregnant, but refused to answer any other question. I was so scared I spent most of the time in my room until my mother made me get a job. I would spend my days in school, work until 9 p.m. and then come home to Mr. A. hiding in my bedroom closet waiting for me. I no longer had the energy or strength to keep trying to avoid him, so I gave in. I started to do whatever he wanted me to do; I was like his little puppet.

After my beautiful daughter was born, things got worst. My family started to ask question again because my daughter looked just like him. They wanted to know who her father was, so I said that her father was the guy I was dating at the beginning of my pregnancy, the one I made sure my family met. They believed me because they saw him around and the timeline added up. One day, I walked in the house and that guy was sitting on my couch. My mother then grabbed my daughter and handed her to him, saying, "Hold your daughter." My heart dropped, and a confused look came on his face. My mother kept pushing the issues, so finally he spoken up. He said, "I liked your daughter and we did date, but no way, this can't be my daughter, because we never had sex." At that moment I knew I had questions to answer, but I managed to get to my room and find a way to avoid the questioning section from him and my mother. She didn't bring the topic back up; she acted like that never happened, so I carried on with life as usual.

My mother seemed to have let the topic go, but my family didn't. They knew, and so did my mother, but she probably didn't want to believe that could happen in her family. My sister would not let up; she wanted me to tell her the truth. However, I was too scared; I asked Mr. A. to tell her, but he refused. He left me to fight that battle alone. My sister and I would get into physical fights over Mr. A., and it got so intense that my sister literally hated me. I was scared every day of my life, not knowing when she was going to pop up or what she was going to say to me or do to me. After a while, I stopped fighting; I didn't have the energy. I knew I was wrong, so I thought maybe I deserved to be treated that way.

As my relationship became more and more tense with my sister, the more comfortable he became, she told the whole family about me. Everyone knew what was going on, so he felt there was no reason for hiding—he could have his cake and eat it too. He started to do things to me in front of my mother and she would ignore it, telling everyone that he was the father of my daughter and making me go places with him in public where he knew my family would see us.

After a while, it became part of my family dynamics. I became the bad person and I am used to get treated wrong; the hurtful part of that treatment, it was coming from my own family. Nobody ever stopped to ask me if I was okay, or how did that happen. Nobody cared how it happened, they just knew that it happened, and it was wrong, therefore, someone needed to take the blame. That person was me, not him... even when he was twice my age. Nobody stopped to protect me.

I was sick of it, so I started to build up my strength again and started avoiding him. I began talking to a guy from work and invited him to my house to watch movies. The cycle continued, but now instead of him attacking the guy, he hit me and busted my lip wide open… I still have the scar to this day. Then, he turned to the guy and asked him if he wanted to be next. Naturally, he took his stuff and walked right out of the front door. I screamed for my mom and she came running down the stairs to rush me to the hospital where I got stitches. She never asked me what happen, or who did this to me…

The next day we carried on like nothing happen. When I went to work to face the guy, he said nothing to me, but everyone there knew what had happened, I could feel the eyes looking at me and hear them whispering about me. After that day, work became another source of discomfort and stress; I didn't even want to be there anymore, so I forced myself to find another job. Nothing in my life was going well. I was stressed out on a daily basis and didn't know what to do or say to change my situation. I began thinking that was how I was going to spend the rest of my life… trapped.

Then, out of nowhere, my luck changed. Mr. A. got arrested and sentenced to jail for 12 months. During that time, I was able to get into my first real relationship with a friend that I met in school, Mr. C. I was starting to separate myself from all of my life troubles and I was actually enjoying life for the first time. I decided to keep him away from my family; I didn't want anything to mess this up. However, that didn't take long before his mother found out that I had a baby, she didn't want me anywhere near her son. He still wanted to be with me anyway, so they argued to the point that he ran away to my house. I wasn't sure if I was ready to deal with something like that, but I opened my arms and let him in. Around the same time, my daughter's father was being released from jail, so I started to prepare myself for the worst. Just like expected, he popped up time after time. But, now it was different because my Mr. C. wasn't scared of him and he wouldn't allow him to touch me. He would stand in front of me. That made me feel so good; I felt that I was finally free from Mr. A.

I guessed wrong. Mr. A. began to watch my house and wait for a night that my boyfriend wasn't spending the night. Oh, yes, I forgot to tell you Mr. C. went back to stay with his mother after she said she was going call the police. One time, Mr. A. broke into my mother's house and… did it again. I never told my boyfriend what happened; I kept it to myself. Soon after my mother moved to another house and I followed her. That house was far away from him, so I was excited. My boyfriend and I were happy. I graduated from high school and started college; everything was going well. Then I ended up pregnant. My world started to spiral out of control again. Everything that was doing good started to crumble. My mother was mad,

Mr. C's mother was mad, my family started to spread rumors, I flunked most of my classes, and he started to cheat on me while I was pregnant... Nothing was going right, but at least Mr. A. was staying away.

As soon as I had my second daughter, I began to feel suffocated. I knew that Mr. C was mistreating me and was abusing me mentally, physically and financially, but I also knew that as long as I stayed with him, Mr. A. would stay away from me. Therefore, I stayed in that toxic relationship for six years. Our relationship was so bad that one time while I was pregnant with his son and thought something was wrong with the baby, he got so mad at me that he stopped what he was doing to take me to the hospital. We argued and fought during the whole way to the hospital, and when we arrived, he bent over, opened the door and pushed me out. The hospital workers rushed to help and took me right into the ER. Thank God that my son was okay.

That man would do unimaginable things to me, but I stayed. I used to convince myself that he loved me until it started to affect my children. He started to get aggressive with my daughter. I didn't care that he was her father, I only cared that he was hurting her and seeing her tears put me into a rage. I flipped out and we got into a huge fight. At that moment, I knew that I had to leave, so I found myself a house and moved while he was at work, leaving everything but my children, clothes, and beds. He found out my address and the cycle started again. He would pop up at my house, interfering me whenever I am talking to another guy. It got to a point where he pulled all the wires out of my car, flatten all my tires, and broke into my house to burn all my clothes. When he jumped though my front window just to get to me, I had to pull a knife on him. I thank God until this day that he had a thick hoodie on because I would have his blood on my hands. That relationship turned me into someone I couldn't even recognize—I was aggressive, angry, violent, and rude to almost all men. I had no respect for no one, including myself.

After that incident, I decided to move again, but to be safe, I had no choice but to move with my father. During the time I lived with my father, we were able to start rebuilding our relationship. My father explained to me that he knew everything he did to my mother and to us was wrong, but he had issues and problems that he was facing and didn't know how to deal with them. He said what he did was the only way he could get any relief from his worries. He also said "I still have a lot of issues, but I'm working on myself". So he wanted to have a second go at a father-daughter relationship. By the time I left my father's house, I felt comfortable enough to start over again. I believed that there was hope for me.

I moved into my new house and started a new relationship for all the right reasons. I wasn't looking for my new boyfriend

Mr. R. to protect me, but to actually love me. Mr. R. didn't stop Mr. C. from harassing me, but the difference was that he stood up for me when I got an order of protection. My new boyfriend wanted to protect me, but I felt I had to learn how to protect myself from abusers. I stood my ground every time he popped up trying to intimidate me. That became a strain in my new relationship because I found a sense of me and I liked it. I didn't want to give up for nothing. I didn't want to look to a man to protect me anymore because they only seem to do the opposite, so I felt if I handed that power over to him I would end up right where I left off.

I liked when I stood in my power, but it seemed to overpower Mr. R, which caused a lot of friction in our relationship. I knew I didn't want that relationship to turn out like my last, so something had to change… what I didn't know was what to do. I started to focus on me and my needs, so I enrolled back into college. I started to reunite with my family, and I cut my hours back at work because I used to work between 60-80 hours as another way to avoid my problems. Then, I began to feel a weight starting to leave off my chest. Everything was getting better. I even was about to finish college a semester early; I was so proud of myself.

After my graduation, I wasn't in a rush to start my new career as a paralegal. My purpose for studying law was to go into the law field so I would be able to help the helpless. I wanted to go into family law to protect children and families from the injustice of this world. During my studies, I quickly figured out that it would take years for me to have the impact that I was seeking, so I started to research a way to help and change lives. I found myself on a website for life coaches. I had heard of life coaches before, but I didn't think it was something real. After doing my research, I was convinced it was something that I could do. I enrolled in Master Coach University. School came easy to me because I love to learn, so I thought it would be a walk in the park for me.

It was totally the opposite. That was the hardest thing I ever had to do; it challenged me in ways that I never expected. We would get weekly scoring from our session and my score was low. I didn't understand why; I couldn't figure what I was doing wrong. So, after the third week, I asked for help for the first time in my life. I asked someone to guide me. That person told me that in order to be successful as a life coach, I had to let go a lot of things and build up my confidence, believe in myself, stop trying to be comfortable and, most importantly, stop hiding and embrace myself . Soon after that conversation, I went from being the student in the back of the classroom to the student in the front of the classroom. I started to open up, honoring my commitments, and in return, I was able to have my clients do to the same during our sessions. My score started to climb quickly; I finally understand the material and what it took for me to be a life coach.

Being a life coach is not about the material; the material are just tools that you use to help people, to make your client's transition easier. In order to even use the material, you have to able to show your client that change is possible, and you accomplish that by coming from a genuine place with your client, sharing your low as well as you high points in your life, and the ways you accomplished your highs. If they feel like you're lying to them or, excuse my language, bullshiting them, you're just going to waste everyone's time. The purpose behind myself going for that certification was to help stop the suffering and to educate. I don't want anyone to go through what I have been though. So, I made a decision to start opening doors in my life that have never been opened. I was about to finish the certification with high scores, and I was asked to speak at the ceremony about my journey and on how I managed to make a shift in my scores. That was a proud moment for me; I was very excited because I was called out for doing something great and I was surrounded with positive energy. At that moment, I wanted everyone to experience that same feeling. The feeling of hope... the feeling that life is possible after tragedy.

After I became a certified life coach, I started to take courses in domestic violence and communication. Also, my sister and I started to rebuild our relationship. I started to confront my issues straight on. There are still moments where I retreat to my own habits of hiding away, but I learned to surround myself with people that don't allow me to stay there. Sometimes old habits find a way to resurface, but if you're aware of what is going on and know how to counteract these bad habits with positive habits and a positive support system, you will be able to fight through. These moments are my hardest, because I feel safe; however, all that does is harming me more than helping me. It took me a long time to get here and I'm trying my very best not to go back to that place again.

To help me, I opened my first business *Let Rose Speak* in 2015 and *All Roses Uniting* in 2017. *Let Rose Speak* gives me a platform to speak out about what happened to me, bring awareness to domestic violence and give people much needed knowledge of hope and change. This has provided me with numerous opportunities to learn and understand people on a different level. *All Roses Uniting* focuses on educating the youth and their family about domestic violence and self-development. I have been able to do a lot of prevention work, and my biggest goal for this business is to stop the generational curse of domestic violence. *All Roses Uniting* was created to stop domestic violence before it happens by educating the youth and their parents about domestic violence and giving them the tools they need to have a fighting chance against domestic violence if they do find themselves in this type of situation.

The creation of these business came from different parts of my desire to help other people. *Let Rose Speak* helps to let people know they don't have to stay locked in a place of silence anymore. You are free to speak about what happens to you and get help. This company is all about bringing awareness and helping those who are victims or survivors of domestic violence.

I have been facing struggles with these businesses because there are still battles that I'm fighting within myself. Thinking that I'm not worthy of greatness, and somewhere in the back of my head, I believe I deserve what happened to me. However, despite of that voice, I keep telling myself that I was placed on this earth for something bigger than myself, that this is my calling and purpose. I keep moving forward regardless. I'm going to continue standing on stage and speaking up for what I believe, and every time I speak, my voice will get a little stronger because I will be further away from the abuse and closer to my calling. I remind myself every day that I no longer live in the place of silence anymore; I'm free and I'm extending my hand out to anyone that may need a helping hand to find their freedom. I was placed on this earth for a reason just like everyone else. We all have purpose. I believe I was chosen to endure all that pain and suffering because God knows my heart; He created me with a heart of forgiveness and understanding. I'm able to forgive those who have wronged me and pray for their recovery and happiness. I'm also about seeing things from the other person's point of view, and I understand that some people are driven by things that can make them have an empowering life, change things because they are feed with greatness. On the other hand, I also know that other people are driven by things that can make them disturbing and disgusting, life-changing things because they were feed with negativity. Every human has their basic to function properly, and when one area is empty, we do whatever is necessary to fill that gap. We can choose to fill that emptiness in either a positive or a negative way. It all depends on what that person sows.

I want to end this chapter with these words...

I know this is not like your traditional inspirational story. I just wanted to give you a look into my real life and real issues. I don't want you to think that once you break through, life becomes some fairytale story because it doesn't. You are still a human, and life will continue to throw things at you that are going to make you want to give up; however, I tell you—don't give up! You have gone so far and worked too hard to give up halfway. If you have to cry, yell, sing, or write it out to get through that moment, do it and then keep on moving!

Chapter 9

Three Keys to Career Success: Action, Accomplishment, & Ability to Pivot

Laura McNeill

Two decades ago, I'd launched my career with hope, dreams, and a lot of enthusiasm. Journalism degree in hand, I managed to land a television news-reporting job with a small CBS affiliate. I began part-time and learned the ropes from the news director, fellow reporters, photographers, and anchors. When I was asked to join the team full time a year later, I was thrilled.

Looking back, it was the most exhilarating and amazing opportunity. I spent six years in the television industry as a reporter, editor, producer, assignment editor, weekend anchor, and morning anchor. I covered house fires, murder trials, county fairs, and car accidents. In my tenure, I reported on elections, one earthquake, and other natural disasters. I was on set, ready to come back from a commercial break, when the two planes hit the World Trade Center.

After six years of working weekends, overnights (2 am – 10 am), and every holiday, it was time for a break. I had a small child and wanted to spend more time seeing my family during the daylight hours. I took a job in pharmaceutical sales—much less glamorous and exciting—but it paid the bills and I was home almost every night.

After four years in the pharmaceutical industry, I was able to stay at home and focus on launching my writing career. I wrote, edited, and published two books, and I was enjoying my two boys, thankful for my life.

Seven years later, my life was upended. After discovering my spouse was unfaithful, I filed for divorce. I endured a brutal, lengthy, and emotionally wrenching break-up. I could not afford to keep the historical home we had so lovingly restored, nor stay in the neighborhood with so many of my close friends. I had little money, no health insurance of my own, and no steady income. The judge assigned to my case ordered the sale of our home, so we were forced to vacate the property in thirty days. *Nightmare* seems the most appropriate word to describe the entire ordeal.

Hundreds of miles away from my closest family and friends, I proceeded to have panic attacks, insomnia, and repeated bouts of absolute terror that my kids and I would be forced to live on the street. I was, at best, confused, exhausted, and uncertain of my next path or goal, let alone how I was supposed to get there. I had to focus on surviving.

Through support from generous souls and a kind mentor from my place of worship, I was able to remind myself I was capable, smart, and resourceful. I put an emergency plan together, as I had to get a job, and I had to get one fast. This was no time for glamour career moves or turning my nose up at hourly work. While I searched for a full-time position, I answered the phone, made appointments at a dietitian's office, and filled in at a local jewelry store. I sold items on eBay and took furniture to a second-hand consignment store. I found a small rental house. And I prayed *a lot*.

As I gained my confidence back, bit by bit, I examined my best options for long-term work. I liked public relations and had lots of experience, but it was not my passion. Reporting and anchoring in the TV news industry, which I'd done six years prior, was fun and exciting, but tough to break back into. In small markets, news jobs paid very little. I'd also worked for four years as a senior pharmaceutical representative, but the job required constant travel, and the industry was in crisis. Friends and acquaintances were being laid off, not hired.

Fast forward six years later…

Today, I'm a book coach, an author, an adjunct professor

at two local universities, and an assistant vice president at a *Fortune 500* company. I've published two suspense novels with HarperCollins Christian and five more under the pen name Lauren Clark. This summer, I will graduate with my Ph.D. from a major research university. I've been fortunate to have these opportunities and have met incredible leaders and mentors along the way.

I've found I'm at my best when I'm able to be creative. I've discovered I love empowering people to discover their talents and reach their goals. Teaching has been immensely rewarding and I truly adore my students. I've discovered a lot about myself, my tenacity, my drive, and my ability to make things happen. Needless to say, the journey from almost-homeless to employed and financially secure was not a straight and narrow path. It's been an expedition.

If you take away anything from my story, I hope that you are inspired to believe it is possible to build a successful, comfortable life out of very little. Though there's no magic formula or secret key to getting everything you want in life; however, I can share how I was able to get my life back.

#1. Action

Any major financial crisis, whether it concerns the loss of a job, loss of a home, divorce, or devastating illness, can easily suffocate the smartest and most talented among us. It is easy to get paralyzed, to decide by not deciding, to give up, and to lock oneself away because of potential public shame or humiliation. Ultimately, I realized the only person who could save me…was me. I had to act, or my entire ship would sink with me and my children on it.

I did take action. I looked at my skill sets and really examined what I could accomplish. I chose to apply for jobs in categories I thought I could manage—marketing, social media, writing, even sales. I rewrote and polished my resume what felt like fifty times, finessed and proofread, all while combing the internet and the community for jobs. I blanketed the market with job applications. I networked. I asked friends of friends about potential opportunities. For the next two months, I did little else but write cover letters, submit resumes, and scan job sites. All told, I applied for more than 120 jobs. Of that, I was invited to three interviews. From one of those interviews, I received a job offer. I was so thankful for that offer that I practically turned cartwheels. I know I cried in relief; I think I collapsed out of sheer joy and managed to sleep a full eight hours for the first time in months.

#2. Accomplishments

For the next year, I worked hard at my job as the social media manager and web designer for a private university. I problem-solved, used my creativity, met deadlines, and did everything I could to support my manager, his manager, and my team. As the months passed, I learned as much as I could about social media management and web design and continued to develop my skills. I took free classes on campus, chatted to faculty members, and spent time talking to students. I volunteered, took part in community activities, and was finally able to breathe.

During that time, though, I wasn't complacent about the future. I researched, read, and networked about career options. I talked to campus leaders and attended events. I did a lot of giving thanks to a power higher than myself. I hugged my boys and enjoyed seeing friends and family. And I continued to dream about what I could accomplish next; I felt deeply that I needed to move into a career that truly tapped into my talents, fulfilled me, and paid the bills.

What made sense? I could write. I was creative. I loved to learn, I liked technology, and I was not (and am not) afraid of hard work. I decided to pursue a degree in Instructional Design and Technology. Before I even filled out any applications, though, I asked myself several hard questions: (1) Will I like this new career field? (2) Can I become proficient at it? (3) Is there room to expand further—on my team, within the university, or within the market place?

I settled on two possible master's degree programs—one completely online and the other a hybrid of face-to-face and online courses. Ultimately, I chose the first, especially after speaking with the program director. She was highly encouraging and thought I'd be a perfect fit for the 18-month program. I applied for scholarships, budgeted my money, and took two classes a semester. It was hard work, many long nights, and it required dedication. I learned a lot, made new friends, and wrote more papers than I can count. At the end of a year and a half, I graduated. And I had a job offer before I was awarded my diploma—an offer that netted a fifteen thousand dollar raise, which more than made up for the nine thousand dollars I paid out of pocket for my program.

#3. Ability to Pivot

While at my new job, again, a university, I had the opportunity to further my education with free and reduced-price classes. I was accepted into the school's Ph.D. program. After one year, I was able to apply for and receive scholarships on the basis of financial need and academic performance. It was a wonderful opportunity. This kept me learning, while at the same time, broadened my skill set in leadership, training, and adult learning.

This was a smaller life pivot. A movement toward other possibilities within a similar field of study. It gave me options— and options are crucial in today's fast-moving career environment. Pivots can be dramatic, but they don't have to rock your entire world. If I had given up my current career entirely and decided to launch a pet-sitting business, that's a big pivot. Rather, I examined what I'd accomplished and looked at where I wanted to go—through the lens of what I knew I enjoyed and in a field that held promise because of the proficiency I'd developed over the years.

When you build from what you know, or what you've seen success in doing, the path, or pivot, to a new rung in your career ladder doesn't seem quite as daunting. Again, I asked myself: (1) Will I enjoy this new career field? (2) Can I become an expert at this new career? (3) Is there room to expand further, either within my team, within the university, or within the market place?

Your Turn

As you probably have seen in the news and online, change is the new normal in business and industry. No longer is there a stigma with moving to a new position or company every two or three years. According to the Employee Benefit Research Institute (EBRI), a person's job tenure now averages only five years. You may decide to pivot because you've mastered your job and want a new challenge. You may see a new position open that is perfectly suited to your personality and life goals. There are no rules here; you can take baby steps or a giant leap. That said, the baby steps allow us to keep growing in a safe place. Start a side hustle and see if you like the new job. Find a mentor in the industry and ask for an informational interview. This is my advice if you decide (or are forced) to make a life change.

Stay Positive

While feelings of uncertainty are normal, it is crucial to move away from feeling desperate, victimized, and without control, especially in the face of professional challenges. It is easy to get stressed and frantic if you are out of your comfort zone. It is real and valid to be concerned or panicked if you are faced with a layoff, a terrible boss, or toxic coworkers. Questions that may be swirling around your mind are, "Am I making the right choices? What will happen next?"

You may be thinking it is easier to stay in your miserable situation. You are correct. It is easier. We rationalize that we should stay in a position because we have been there five, fifteen, or twenty years. However, the cost of doing nothing is a high price to pay. Staying stuck in a job when you are very unhappy often leads to exhaustion, physical illness, and career burnout. You have a choice. You don't have to stay for another year. This is the universe and your intuition telling you it is time to move on.

Take time in a quiet place to search your soul. Breathe. Lean on friends who love and support you. Learn to be accountable, responsible, and capable—viewing the change as a new path— and as you travel, you will learn and grow. To the best of your ability, turn the negative into a positive. Use this opportunity to achieve the success you deserve.

Instead of dwelling on what you'll lose, imagine a career that makes you feel challenged, happy, and fulfilled. If that vision looks, feels, and sounds better, shift your efforts away from focusing on sunk costs and look toward your new trajectory.

Take Action

Evaluate Your Passions. This may seem obvious, but building a new career or making a life change means deeply examining the true interests in your life. What lights you up and gets you excited? What could you do all day that doesn't seem like work? What do friends and family always praise you about? Take a detailed personal inventory of those activities, interests, and hobbies.

Rather than overthinking job changes, look for low-risk, smaller opportunities that you can accomplish online and in the few hours. Join a local Meet Up. Attend library meetings on topics you love. Create a LinkedIn account and politely message people who hold jobs that seem like a good possibility for you in the future. Volunteer. Interview interesting people. Ask questions and explore unique professions that interest you. Tell everyone you know that you are looking for a new career. Take classes on Coursera, Lynda.com, or Udemy. Keep updated resumes in your car and in your bag or briefcase. Create business cards to hand out. In the process, you may make valuable connections you would not have gained otherwise.

Action is key. Once you begin down a new path, stay committed. It can often take months—or years—to see major change. Above all else, avoid negative people and situations. Positivity and energy are contagious, so surround yourself and network with individuals and leaders who believe in you and share your goals.

Tally Accomplishments

Keep track of what you are learning, and if a friend offers to help, consider taking the person up on it. True professionals know they have gaps in their knowledge and skill sets. Most leaders also work diligently to close these spaces. Those who do, succeed much more often than those who ignore the opportunities and possibilities in front of them. There are many free courses online, so take advantage of them and add those to your resume. If you volunteer, add that to your resume. Employers love a well-rounded candidate who is motivated, curious, and dedicated to self-improvement.

Build Your Village

Work hard at developing an empowering, engaged community of colleagues who can help pave your way to success. Successful professionals know they cannot achieve their goals and dreams in a void; they must establish and build mutually beneficial relationships. Those solid bonds and partnerships can help propel your career forward. Know that not everyone may want to help, and that is okay. Move on to the next person and the next one, always in a spirit of collaboration. What can you bring to the table? Sometimes energy and excitement is enough in the beginning.

Always build these relationships on trust, honesty, and integrity. Remember, sometimes it's what you do, not what you say, that speaks the loudest. Once you have established yourself, it is time to pay it forward and offer a helping hand to the next woman who needs encouragement and advice. You can be that person.

Prepare to Pivot

Talk to those friends and mentors about times when they decided to pivot or make a career change. Ask them what they did right and what they would change if they had the opportunity to repeat the process. A career change can be a daunting endeavor, but it helps to remind yourself daily of exactly what you want and where you'd like to be in a year or five years. Write it down in a journal. Blog about your goals. Repeat a mantra like, "I've got this." Talk to friends about it. Talking about dreams and goals puts those words out into the universe.

Above all, be open to new people and possibilities. The next person you meet may hold the key to the future you. So, instead of letting fear and anxiety take hold, stay positive, and remember that you hold the key to your future. Remind yourself that the unknown world holds endless potential.

Chapter 10

Leadership – an Inner Journey

Dr. Catherine Hayes

I can't think of a time in my life when I wasn't in some kind of leadership role. However, it never occurred to me that I was a natural born leader.

I think this is true for many of us. We fall naturally into leadership positions—in school, in our families, and in our communities—not because we feel called to lead, but because we can no longer sit by and watch others struggle to lead effectively.

Often, it's a failure in leadership that catapults us into a leading role. This was certainly what happened for me. After witnessing exemplary leadership as well as numerous failures in leadership over the course of my academic career, I began to understand that leadership is something that needs tending to, not something that a person can simply claim once and own forever. I was intrigued by how leadership style influences outcomes, and came to believe that an effective leadership style is something a person can learn and develop, even if they are not, at first glance, a natural leader.

In my career in public health dentistry and as an educator at Harvard and Tufts University, I was repeatedly called into leadership roles. I also had plenty of experience in dealing with lackluster leadership and its very tangible repercussions. What I came to realize is that being a good leader is different from being a "boss" or a manager. Management and leadership may often be lumped under the same umbrella, but they are not the same thing. Management is an intellectual skill set, but leadership is related to one's character. There are no hard metrics to it; I have not come across a single definition that encompasses all aspects of effective leadership. We simply know it when we see it, and even more when we feel it. Inspiring leaders are those who bring out the best in those around them, and do so with integrity, courage and grace.

Despite the fact that great leadership isn't easily defined in hard terms, it isn't elusive. In my workshops, I often ask participants to bring to mind an individual who has inspired them in their personal or professional life, and jot down two or three qualities about that person which stand out as "leadership" qualities. Invariably, the words which emerge are "integrity," "respect," "kindness," "honesty," "compassion," "a good listener," "believed in me," and the like.

In essence, being a good leader begins with being a good person—a "do as I do" kind of person. When people in positions of leadership don't demonstrate the essential core qualities listed above, and instead fall into a "do as I do" mentality, it trickles down to impact the lives of individuals within the organization, and the structural integrity of the organization itself. Great leadership can help people show up as their best selves, but poor leadership can easily empower a culture of mediocrity, dishonesty, and bullying.

In a recent report released by Gallup, titled The State of the *American Workplace*, it was estimated that between $450 and $600 billion are lost each year in US corporations because of lack of leadership (which includes lack of communication, lack of clarity, etc.). What this tells me is that real leaders are in short supply, and that they are desperately needed. People need leaders whom they can respect, admire, and emulate. When such people are not present in our organizations and government, chaos (financial and otherwise) ensues.

The more I learned about this concept, the more I understood that I could use my knowledge and skills to help cultivate positive leadership qualities in others. So, I embarked on a journey to deeply understand leadership development.

In my mind, everyone has inherent leadership potential.

Whether we aspire to be effective leaders within our families, in our communities, or in the workplace, we must start the journey within ourselves. To have the positive impact on others that we desire, we need to connect with the core qualities within us which make us unique, which uphold our integrity, and which make others want to follow us. Also, we must continue to cultivate and refine these qualities even after we've attained whatever position we are reaching toward.

To me, the most important aspect of effective leadership is self-awareness. We must understand ourselves fully, so we can be in greater control of our actions, reactions, decisions, and attitudes. We need to know what triggers us, what unconscious fears are at play, and which habits and repetitive patterns get in our way. Then, we need to learn to stop judging these things in ourselves, so we can optimize our strengths while showing up in a more compassionate way for others.

One of the most important tools I've gained on my own inner journey and in the work I do today in the leadership development field is the Enneagram. The modern Enneagram is a synthesis of ancient wisdom and modern psychology. It is a very rich system and a powerful vehicle for transformation that goes far beyond its popularity as a personality-typing tool.

The term Enneagram is derived from the Greek words *ennea*, which means nine, and *gram*, which means something written. The nine personality types are arranged around a symbol, which shows the interactions among the types. Understanding our Enneagram personality type can help us to unlock a greater understanding of who we really are underneath our patterns of behavior.

As my teachers, Don Riso and Russ Hudson, often said, "Our Enneagram type is not who we are, it is who we are not." This speaks to the transformational potential of the Enneagram—which, if used correctly, can guide us into a deeper understanding of our true nature. By bringing greater awareness and presence to our personality structures, we can wake up to our truth, expand our field of conscious choice around our attitudes and behaviors, and live more authentically by cultivating our positive qualities and values. We can also use the Enneagram as a tool in our relationships to understand those with whom we live and work, and deepen our mutual connections to our shared values and goals.

Understanding our Enneagram personality type can help us unlock our potential as leaders, and also see what holds us back from being effective and impactful in our chosen sphere. When we understand our inherent strengths as well as our potential limitations, we enliven the leader within us. Approached with integrity and curiosity, the Enneagram can bring a level of self-knowledge that is unparalleled.

To help get you started on this inner journey of leadership, I've created brief descriptions of the nine Enneagram types and their leadership styles. If you haven't already done an assessment to determine your Enneagram type, don't worry—chances are, you will be able to self-determine your type simply because you resonate strongly with one or two of these descriptions.

- **Type Ones** know how to get the job done, and done well. There is little room for error. They have the ability to see what is needed in order to make things right because their focus is always on creating perfection. The Type One has a strong need for things to be neat, orderly and perfect, and they can be harsh critics of themselves and others. This can create challenges as they tend to be taskmasters and have difficulty delegating. Before Type Ones become self-aware, their inner critics can literally run their lives, pushing them to try to live up to high and often unrealistic expectations. Things can become even more challenging when Ones put the weight of these expectations onto others, who (in their eyes) inevitably fall short. Freedom from their personality comes through letting go of the need for everything to be perfect, and entering a state of trust that others have valuable input. This relieves the Type One of the burden of having to do it all since nobody can live up to their expectations.

- **Type Twos** are openhearted and altruistic leaders. They can sense into the needs of individuals and the group. The challenge for the Type Two is that they are natural "people-pleasers," and are inclined to behaviors like flattery and over-generosity.

They also may have trouble pointing out where things need to change. This can lend itself to a false sense of confidence within their teams. Also, putting the needs of others before their own can lead them to dismiss their own needs and wants, which can lead to resentment. Before they become self-aware, Type Twos can get caught in their need to be seen as helpful by manipulating people and situations to feed their unconscious need for approval. They can be possessive and prideful. Freedom from their personality patterns comes from trusting that they are lovable and worthy and that they do not have to constantly prove it by sacrificing themselves to others. Sometimes, it's more loving to hold people accountable!

- **Type Threes,** as leaders, are success-oriented and often take center stage. Type Threes are authentic, genuine, inspiring, self-accepting, and can be wonderful mentors, and you can often find them in leadership roles. However, the challenge for the Type Three is an unconscious belief that they are worthless; therefore, they are always trying to prove themselves to others. They become highly effective and productive, and can easily slip into overachieving in their careers at the expense of their personal relationships and even their health. Freedom from their personality patterns comes from connecting with their hearts deeply, and accepting that their value comes from who they are and not what they do. When this happens, Threes no longer crave the limelight, and can become valuable co-contributors to the team and community.

• **Type Fours** are highly intuitive and creative, but often struggle with fitting into their families, their organizations, or society at large. They have an underlying belief that they are somehow flawed, and often struggle with melancholy and moodiness which can influence their leadership. They see themselves as different, unique and special; this sense of being different becomes an identity for the Type Four, and as such it is difficult for them to let go of their story. Freedom from their personality patterns comes when they let go of the belief that they are not enough, and allow themselves to step into a state of belonging to a group, team, family, or organization. When they do this, Type Fours can accept themselves and appreciate their strengths of appreciation of beauty, creativity, and intuition.

• **Type Fives** are often reluctant leaders, as they are more comfortable staying in the background and observing every detail of what is happening in the organization. They can appear detached, because they like to figure things out in their heads before coming forward with a solution. At their best, Type Fives are extremely bright and compassionate and pos-sess the gift of clarity, however if they lack self-awareness they can be extremely detached from their emotions, and have a fear of connecting with others due to their fears of inadequacy. They often become experts in one specific area, and find their connection to the group through their expertise. Freedom from their personality patterns comes when they feel confident in connecting to the world and their hearts. When this happens, listen to them! They are gifted and brilliant, and the clarity that they bring to a team is unsurpassed.

• **Type Sixes** are natural leaders, but rarely see themselves as such. They often lead by building consensus and dutifully carrying out the tasks of their group. They are the glue that holds the team together. They are excellent troubleshooters, and have a plan for every possible worst-case scenario; therefore, the team relies on them for answers. At their best, Type Sixes lead from a place of trusting others to support them, which allows them to pay attention to the details that need to be addressed in order for the team to be successful. Their challenge is that, when they struggle with a lack of trust in the support around them, they can become suspicious, skeptical, pessimistic, and indecisive. Freedom from their personality patterns comes from letting go of the need to look to others for answers, and trusting their own inner authority.

• **Type Sevens,** as leaders, are visionaries, endlessly generating new ideas. Operationalizing their ideas can be challenging, as they do not like to be mired in detail and loathe boredom. They see endless possibilities in life and often pursue numerous activities and experiences and find it difficult to slow down. They embody joy and freedom, and can be enthusiastic about recruiting others to follow their vision. However, they may fear that they are missing out on experiences by sticking to one track or task, and so may pursue many activities and experiences with abandon. Their insatiability with experiences and new ideas can lead to indecision, chaotic thinking, and stuckness. Freedom from their personality patterns comes from appreciating their experiences, staying present, sticking with what is needed to bring their ideas to fruition, and no longer looking for excitement and fulfillment by endlessly pursuing new opportunities. When this self-awareness blossoms, they become satisfied with their life and work and feel a sense of contentment.

• **Type Eights,** at their best, are strong leaders with magnanimous hearts. They provide for the underdog, and have a wonderful capacity to help others feel safe and protected. They are often referred to as "The Boss" or "The Challenger," as they have an innate need to control. When this control is threatened, they can become willful, demanding, and vengeful. They may even engage in bullying. Freedom from their personality patterns comes from letting go of the need to be in control in all situations, and instead becoming more openhearted and vulnerable—which, in turn, allows the gift of true strength to emerge.

• **Type Nines** want to keep the peace. At their best, they are grounded, serene and whole, truly embodying Being. They are the known as "The Peacemakers." However, their need for peace and harmony at all costs can result in them ignoring a sinking ship. They rarely express anger; instead, their need to hold onto a peaceful connection with others can result in them becoming withdrawn and disengaged at the first sign of potential conflict. When they are unaware of these tendencies within themselves, their teams can become frustrated with their inability to deal with challenging situations. Outside of times of conflict or challenge, on the other hand, people generally experience Type Nines as easygoing, kind, and fun to be around. Freedom from their personality patterns comes when Type Nines embrace reality in all its beautiful messiness, embrace all of their emotions, and become truly self-accepting. When this awareness occurs, they can lead with a peaceful and grounded style.

When we determine our personality type, we can also tap into our innate leadership style, and mitigate some of the challenges that may be holding back our teams, organizations, or families. Chances are, after reading the above descriptions, you can already see where your strengths lie, and where you may need to do some work.

Cultivating great leadership within ourselves starts with simple observation. What are our habitual patterns? What situations and feelings do we avoid? What is our style when it comes to conflict management? And where are our personalities or our lack of self-awareness creating friction for ourselves and others?

Leadership, like all other things that truly matter, is an

inside job. When you go within, and get in touch with the core qualities that make you unique and capable, you will start to shine, no matter what role you're currently in. My wish for you is that you become more of who you truly are, so you can lead authentically, and create a trickle-down effect of integrity, honesty, and compassion wherever you go.

Women helping Women - Creating a Path for Future Leaders

How does a woman succeed? By using every inch of her reserves, I say. She will have to muster every single resource to make her career and life goals a reality. As I embarked on my journey of discovery into the lives of the ten women in this book, I realized that a woman would rarely have the luxury of having adequate support, opportunities, and mentoring come her way. She will have to carve her path and fight for every bit of her success. The journey upwards and forwards for a woman has so many hurdles that initiating a career and sustaining it may seem an impossible task. The world is hardly an ideal place for a woman to live in and workplaces even less so. However, ten women did it—they climbed out of despair and hopelessness and created a world for them to shine in. More significantly, a world that allowed more than one woman to reveal her inner goddess.

Workplaces all over the world are just beginning to grasp the problem of the gender gap and unequal pay for men and women. Gender parity and fair compensation is merely a distant dream as of now. Inclusiveness and diversity are added dimensions of a workplace that embraces women, especially in leadership roles. The glaring question is—how do we get there? One way is to talk to women leaders who are at the forefront of their careers, such as with the ten amazing women whose stories I've told in this book, to understand the dimensions of the problem. Interacting with these incredible role models helped me gain insight into the blood, sweat, and tears that go into the creation of a woman leader.

I have come to understand that it is possible to create an environment that encourages women to take the reins of their life into their own hands. The biggest strength that a woman can depend on is herself. There is no substitute for mental grit and determination to change one's surroundings. However, what if you are stuck in swampy mud? What if struggling makes it harder for you to get out of your circumstances? That is when women helping women comes in. The day a woman decides to get out of her personal rut does not translate into meaningful change for other women or society at large. A woman leader is a game changer when she extends a helping hand to the women who are looking for direction and opportunity. The gender gap in workplaces can be addressed when a woman leader walks the path and shows the way to others.

Hiring other women, creating teams with adequate represen-
tation of women, and providing opportunities for women to
advance in their careers at the same pace as men, can be the
way forward—especially when a woman is at the helm and in
a position to help other women.

Often, women who advance in their careers are too busy
struggling with their work and personal life balance to see the
bigger picture. If everyone is climbing up the ladder, someone
needs to look down and clear a path for others following in
their way. It is possible to create a workplace that encourages
women workers to establish themselves and ascend in their
career graphs. This may be done by generating specific workplace policies that ensure significant women are employed.
Once women are employed, the workplace needs to be a
safe place where a woman can work without fear or stress of
harassment or unequal treatment. Again, specific guidelines
and women resource teams need to be in place to ensure that
women retain their jobs.

Women are naturally placed into situations that involve
childcare and rearing within a family. That directly translates
into an increased burden on a woman at the cost of a fulfilling
career. Employers, especially women in leadership roles, understand these issues and can create workspaces that allow for a
parental leave of sufficient duration, childcare options within
the workplace, and work-at-home options for women so that

they are motivated to continue working outside the home. The boundaries need to be expanded regarding what constitutes a woman's job; for example, is bringing up a child the primary responsibility of a mother? The answer to this lies in redefining the problem. Dividing home chores, and bringing up kids is a joint responsibility of mothers and fathers, and employers need to address that by giving maternal and paternal leaves. Similarly, the issue of gender and pay gap is a problem for society, not just for women. Men, too, need to be engaged as well so that it is the joint effort of both sexes to balance and support each other at home and at work. The attitude and biases of men towards women colleagues also have to be modified, and their inherent prejudices stripped away through information, discussion, and becoming a part of the conversation on women empowerment.

Even with the best of workplace scenarios and opportunities, a woman may not be able to achieve as much as she wants. Society and childhood trauma place immense pressure on a woman to conform to stereotypes—women are left wishing to be thinner, prettier, or better mothers. The burden of expectations—within and without—begin to close the walls around a woman and limit the dimensions of her expectations from herself. This is a battle a woman has to win for herself. Many of the women I spoke to during the compilation of this book talked about how difficult it was to silence their inner shaming voice. How can you move forward if you've tied yourself down with chains of your own making? You have to let go of what the world wants from you, to own what you wish for yourself. By reading, talking, and following the journey of women who have transformed their lives and dared to make the change needed to achieve more than they ever thought possible.

We're getting there. Progress may be slow and a long time coming, but it is steady. As long as women are willing to share their stories and make other women feel like they are not alone, progress towards ownership of their life will continue. Women's empowerment is the empowerment of an individual, a society, a home, and a workplace. It all starts from one woman and her resolve to change. I hope this book and its real-life heroines inspire you to make the transformation you've always needed in your life, just like it helped me look at mine with new eyes. Cheers to a new you!

FABULOUS CAREER CHANGE Mini-Workbook

Laura McNeill

Author & Book Coach

www.lauramcneill.com

YOUR CAREER CHANGE PURPOSE

Before you change careers, you must clearly understand your purpose. Think about and answer the following questions:

Why do I want a career change? What am I seeking? What do I love doing that never seems like work? What career would help make my life truly fabulous?

How could this career improve my life, help my community, or make the world a better place?

_____

_____

_____

_____

_____

_____

_____

_____

_____

_____

_____

_____

_____

_____

_____

YOUR DREAM CAREER

The best way to begin taking steps toward your career change goal is to begin with your dream.

Describe your ideal career. Something fun and fabulous! What job would you have? Who would you interact with? Alone or with a team? Work from home or in the office? Travel? Projects?

_____

_____

_____

_____

_____

_____

_____

_____

Now, list the skills, talents, and experience you already have, especially those matching your ideal career.

_____

_____

_____

_____

_____

_____

_____

JOB BRAINSTORM

Thinking about your skills, talents, and experience, brainstorm and write down a list of -7 possible jobs that could put you on the path to your ideal career.

1. _____

2. _____

3. _____

4. _____

5. _____

6. _____

7. _____

Identify 3 small steps you can take today toward your ideal career:

1. _____

2. _____

3. _____

Identify 3 skills you could learn (a free online course, training, internship, volunteer work, etc.) that could help put you on a path toward a fabulous career.

1. _____

2. _____

3. _____

THE FUTURE YOU!

Who can help you make your ideal career happen? (People already working in your ideal career field, connected to it, or a career recruiter, etc.). Write their names below. Promise yourself you will ask for their guidance.

1. _____

2. _____

3. _____

Who is in your "village?" Name 3 people who will love and cheer you on during this career change (family, friends, colleagues, etc.).

1. _____

2. _____

3. _____

Now, make it official. Make a promise to yourself that you will achieve your fabulous career goal. Beginning with "Today, I will…" write 2-3 sentences you can use as daily motivation to go after your dreams.

Today, I will

_____

_____

_____

_____

Dr. Catherine Hayes
Leadership Coach
Consulting & Author
www.catherinehayescoaching.com

Leslie Thomas Flowers
Bestselling Author
Speaker & Perfomance Catalyst
www.leslie-flowers.com

Trina Ramsey
Author & Life Coach
Founder of the
Just Do You Institute
www.mycoachtrina.com

Kirsten Blakemore
MA, CPCC, ACC, CHC
& Senior Consulting Partner
at Partners in Leadership
www.partnersinleadership.com

Rose Jones
Founder of Let Rose Speak
& Accountability Coach
www.letrosespeak.com

Maggie Georgopoulos
Bestselling Author
Consultant & Speaker
www.magsinspires.com

Rhonda Kinard
Author, Speaker
CEO of A Life Ignited, LLC
www.alifeignited.com

Laura McNeill
Researcher, Educator
& Bestselling Author
www.lauramcneill.com

Tracie L. James
Author, Speaker
Writer & Consultant
www.tracieljames.com

Divya Parekh
Business Coach, Speaker
& Bestselling Author
www.divyaparekh.com

The 3 C's of life: Choices. Chances. Changes.

You must make a choice to take a chance or your life will never change.
Naghilia Desravines

www.ingramcontent.com/pod-product-compliance
Lightning Source LLC
Chambersburg PA
CBHW070717220326
41598CB00024BA/3196